MW00812994

Disaster Ready in 14 Steps

Emergency Survival Guide for New Preppers

ALEX KINLEY

Copyright © 2023 by DavidsonEventures, Inc, Eau Claire, Wisconsin. All rights reserved.

No part of this publication may be reproduced or transmitted in any form or by any means, electronic or mechanical, including photocopying, recording, or by any information storage and retrieval system, without permission in writing from the publisher. Unless otherwise noted, all images, figures, templates, and designs are copyright © 2023 by DavidsonEventures, Inc. However, we want you and your community to be Prepared! Copies of this and other *Disaster Ready*™ books may be available in bulk at a discount. Contact us at info@canvenia.com for more information.

Published by Canvenia
A division of DavidsonEventures, Inc.
P.O. Box 1353, Eau Claire, Wisconsin, 54701, USA

Limit of Liability/Disclaimer of Warranty: The Publisher and the author make no representations or warranties with respect to the accuracy or completeness of the contents of this work and specifically disclaim all warranties, including without limitation warranties of fitness for a particular purpose. No warranty may be created or extended by sales or promotional materials. The advice and strategies contained herein may not be suitable for every situation. This work is sold with the understanding that the publisher is not engaged in rendering medical, legal, or other professional advice or services. If professional assistance is required, the services of a competent professional person should be sought. Neither the publisher nor the author shall be liable for damages arising herefrom. The fact that an individual, organization, or website is referred to in this work as a citation and/or potential source of further information does not mean that the author or the Publisher endorses the information the individual, organization or website may provide or recommendations they/it may make. Further, readers should be aware that Internet websites listed in this work may have changed or disappeared between when this work was written and when it was read.

Unless otherwise indicated, all Scripture quotations are from World English Bible. Scripture quotations marked (ESV) are from The ESV® Bible (The Holy Bible, English Standard Version®), copyright © 2001 by Crossway, a publishing ministry of Good News Publishers. Used by permission. All rights reserved.

Paperback ISBN: 978-1-958143-21-6
Hardcover ISBN: 978-1-958143-22-3
Ebook ISBN: 978-1-958143-23-0

This book is dedicated to my family, neighbors, and community.

May we be ready for adversity when we are faced with it and come out stronger!

Welcome to *Disaster Ready*!

You will learn a lot fast as you complete the steps in this book. Below is a link to our FREE Wallet-Sized Emergency Contacts form (8.5 x 11 inches). It prints perfectly-sized for your wallet.

When carrying this Emergency Contacts form, each family member can be connected.

Learn more and download by visiting the link below!

Wallet-Sized Emergency Contacts (PDF)
www.Canvenia.com/Wallet-Card

Table of Contents

Introduction

"And let them gather all the food of these good years that are coming and store up grain under the authority of Pharaoh for food in the cities and let them keep it. That food shall be a reserve for the land against the seven years of famine that are to occur in the land of Egypt so that the land may not perish through the famine."

– Genesis 41:35-36

The passage above retells an event in history that occurred in Egypt. A man named Joseph effectively led the effort to prepare his community for hardship. Four thousand years later, we face our own uncertainties. Whether it's a powerful hurricane, a devastating earthquake, a raging wildfire, a widespread blackout, or a global pandemic, calamities can strike at any time. Being ready to face these challenges head-on can make an impactful difference for you, your family, and your community. This book simplifies preparedness for many different disasters. By following the 14 Steps outlined within, you will become ready to face most natural and man-made disasters.

If you have a family, this book will also empower you to turn scary possibilities into an adventure of preparation. As parents, teaching your kids how to prepare is just one more opportunity to bond with your children and help them stand taller, with more courage. Preparedness can be fun if you prepare together. Let's face it, we are stronger when we help each other grow stronger. This book will help you keep that process simple. You will see "family" referred to a lot throughout this book. Please know that you can substitute "roommates" or "yourself" instead.

Whether you live in a bustling city, a rural area, or anywhere in between, this guide is designed to be adaptable to your specific living environment. Are you in a desert or the tundra? It is important that you follow the steps provided. There is a reason for the order, to help you prepare as efficiently as possible. That said, you will not need all the information. Some sections are dedicated to categories of emergencies for which you have no risk. For example, cold-weather emergencies are not a concern to everyone. You may have no children or no elderly persons in your life. As you turn the pages, you'll put together your own emergency plan following the 14 Steps provided. Use the material that pertains to you and make these steps work for your unique situation. You are your best help.

Now, more than ever, we need to arm ourselves with knowledge and preparation. Relying solely on external assistance during a disaster can be risky, as emergency services may be overwhelmed or delayed in reaching you. Being prepared for disasters encourages self-reliance, ensuring that you can take care of your basic needs until help arrives. In times of crisis, fear can lead to chaos and confusion. If you and your family are prepared, you are less likely to succumb to panic because you have a clear plan of action and the necessary supplies to sustain yourself. This not only enhances personal safety but also fosters a sense of calm in the community.

Get ready to feel empowered as you work through the steps to become prepared for any disaster you might face.

*"The beginning is the most important
part of the work."*

— Plato

Know Your Risks and Resources

"It does not do to leave a live dragon out of your calculations if you live near one."

– *The Hobbit* by J.R.R. Tolkien

Action Items

- ✓ Identify your local risks.
- ✓ Identify local organizations or resources and learn the scope of their service in emergencies.
- ✓ Review the "Big Picture" of various disasters.

Before studying the specifics of emergency preparation, it is important for you to identify which disasters threaten you and your community, so you can have a focused strategy for your preparedness plan. To do this with full information, community resources, such as the local Red Cross, Police Department, or Fire Department can help you identify which of the following disasters threaten your community. Make a list of these resources and call a few of them to learn more about their support regarding emergency preparedness.

REFERENCE LIST: CONSIDER YOUR LOCAL RISKS

Provided below is a list of potential disasters. By the time you reach the end of this book, you will know how you would respond to each of the risks that threaten your community. For now, **check, mark, or otherwise note the topics that may relate to you:**

- **Natural Disasters:**
  - Earthquakes
  - Hurricanes/Tropical Cyclones
  - Tornadoes
  - Floods
  - Wildfires
  - Severe Winter Storms
  - Thunderstorms
  - Tsunamis

- **Man-Made Incidents:**
  - Industrial Accidents
  - Chemical Spills/Hazmat Incidents
  - Terrorism/Acts of Violence

- **Health Emergencies:**
  - Disease Outbreaks

- **Technological and Infrastructure Failures:**
  - Power Outages
  - Water Supply Disruptions

- **Climate-Related Events:**
  - Extreme Heatwaves
  - Droughts
  - Heavy Snowfall/Ice Storms

- **Home-Based Emergencies:**
  - Residential Fires
  - Gas Leaks
  - Carbon Monoxide Leaks

- **Environmental Disruptions:**
  - Air Pollution
  - Water Pollution

- **Radiation and Nuclear Incidents:**
  - Radiological Contamination

- **Food and Water Shortages:**
  - Food Supply Disruptions

While this list covers a wide variety of emergencies, the goal is for you to identify those that are potential risks for you. You may have a solid understanding of community-specific risks, but there are good reasons to reach out to one or more organizations who can shed light on unique risks your community faces, such as proximity to industrial facilities, fault lines, or flood-prone areas. Ask about the capabilities and limitations of local emergency services, including first responders and evacuation plans. You'll want to identify local resources and support available in your community.

REFERENCE LIST: LOCAL RESOURCES

Local organizations have the potential to be a boon in your time of need. Your task is to learn, from one or more of these resources, which types of emergencies your community has experienced in the past.

1. **Red Cross and Red Crescent Societies:** These organizations are known for their disaster response efforts, providing emergency shelter, medical assistance, and disaster relief services. They also provide support in prevention, preparedness, and training, such as with first aid and hands-only CPR.

2. **Local Fire Departments:** Firefighters often play a critical role in disaster response, helping with search and rescue, medical aid, and managing hazardous materials. They also have community outreach efforts and can answer questions you may have about your local risks.

3. **Local Police Departments:** Police personnel are often involved in disaster response by providing security, managing traffic, and assisting with evacuations. These departments often have a person designated for community outreach and can answer questions you have about past and potential scenarios.

4. **Food Banks:** Local food banks may step up during disasters to provide food and supplies to those in need, especially if regular access to food is disrupted. But don't count on them immediately after a disaster. For this, you will need your own personal "portable emergency kit," which you will learn how to assemble in Step 6.

5. **Animal Shelters and Rescue Groups:** These organizations work to rescue and care for pets and other animals affected by disasters, ensuring their safety and well-being.

6. **Faith-Based Organizations:** Many churches, mosques, synagogues, and temples offer assistance during disasters, serving their community with shelter, food, and other support.

7. **Utility Companies:** Utility companies work to restore essential services, like electricity, water, and gas following disasters.

CONSIDER BIG-PICTURE OVERVIEWS OF VARIOUS DISASTERS

By thoroughly understanding the different types of disasters and the specific risks in your area, you'll be better prepared to assess your vulnerabilities and develop a tailored emergency preparedness plan. This knowledge is the foundation upon which you can build a resilient and adaptable approach to disaster readiness. While the scenarios below are by no means exhaustive, they can help you get a sense of when to leave your home and when to hunker down. Review the following pages to see the big picture for these various emergencies. Skip over the ones that do not pertain to you.

In the next chapter, you'll begin drafting your Family Emergency Plan.

FIGURE 1.1: Infographic on Home Fire Preparedness
(Canvenia, 2023)

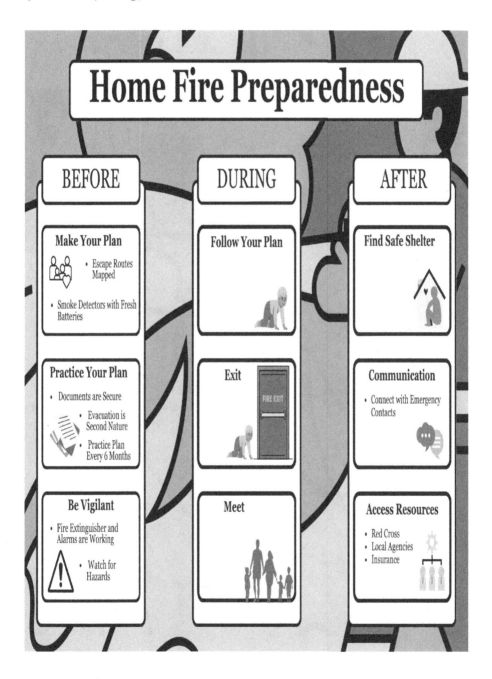

FIGURE 1.2: Infographic on Wildfire Preparedness (Canvenia, 2023)

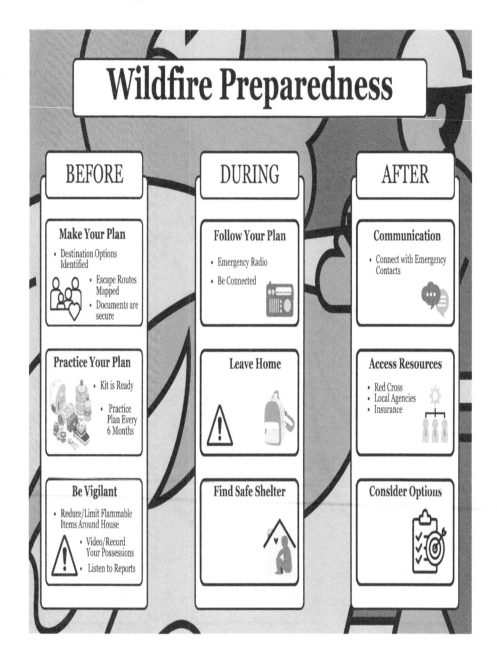

FIGURE 1.3: Infographic on Flood Preparedness
(Canvenia, 2023)

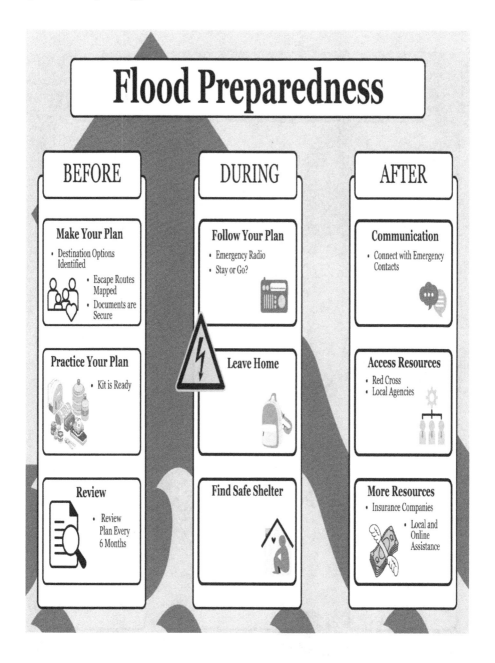

FIGURE 1.4: Infographic on Earthquake Preparedness (Canvenia, 2023)

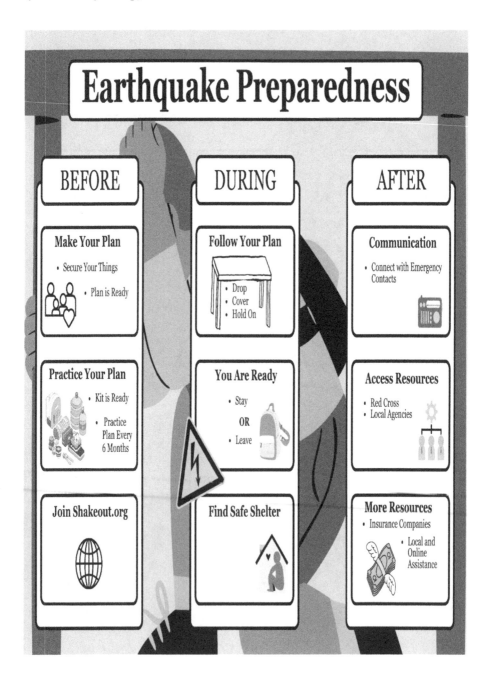

FIGURE 1.5: Infographic on Tropical Storm Preparedness

(Canvenia, 2023)

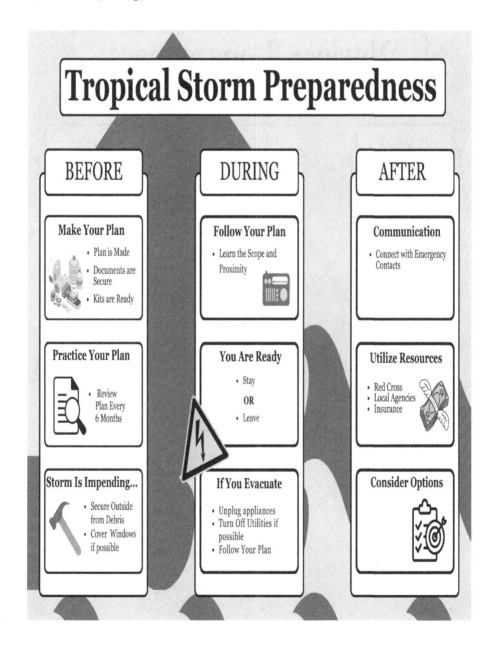

FIGURE 1.6: Infographic on Nuclear Preparedness (Canvenia, 2023)

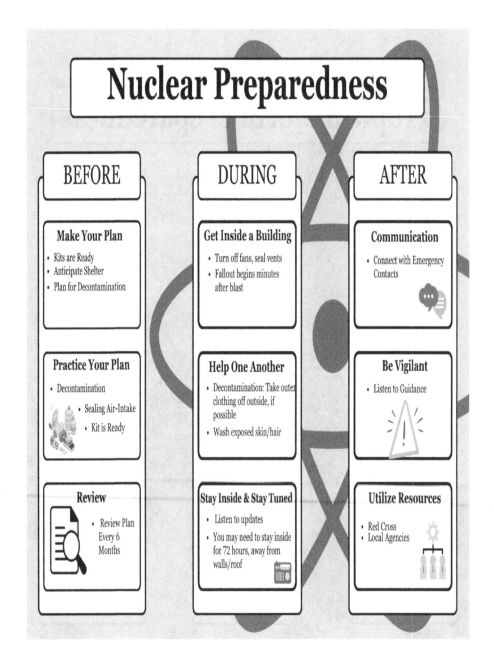

FIGURE 1.7: Infographic on General Preparedness
(Canvenia, 2023)

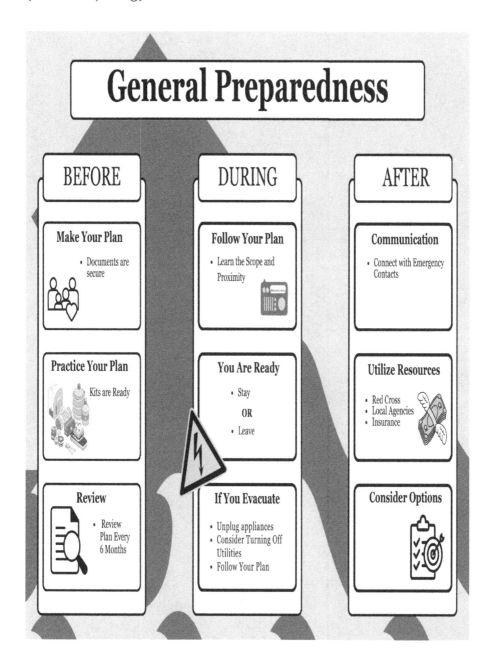

Make Your Family Emergency Plan

"Keep your face always toward the sunshine—
and shadows will fall behind you."

– Walt Whitman

Action Items

- ✓ Fill out your Family Emergency Plan Template (available below).
- ✓ Make a copy of this Plan for your Go-Bag.

A Family Emergency Plan is an essential document you put together that outlines how your family will respond and stay safe during various disasters and emergencies. A well-thought-out plan does not have to be hard or time consuming to create. Look at the form below. Notice how the components provide you with security in various ways.

By the time you have completed the 14 Steps outlined in this book, you will know when to leave your home and when to stay home. You will have the items to get you by for a minimum of three days and up to two weeks. You may certainly plan for more days if you like. It all starts by completing the Family Emergency Plan.

In the next chapter, you'll learn about the importance of gathering your essential documents and cataloging your valuable items in the event of an emergency.

FIGURE 2.1: Family Emergency Plan – CONTACTS

(Canvenia, 2023)

our FAMILY EMERGENCY PLAN

FAMILY: _____   YEAR: (20_____) 1○ 2○ 3○ 4○ 5○

FAMILY MEMBERS

PICTURE ATTACHED

NAME	DOB	PHONE #	EMAIL	SOCIAL MEDIA	
_____	____	_____	_____	_____	☐
_____	____	_____	_____	_____	☐
_____	____	_____	_____	_____	☐
_____	____	_____	_____	_____	☐

PET NAME	TYPE	COLOR	REGISTRATION #	
_____	_____	_____	_____	☐
_____	_____	_____	_____	☐

HAVE MORE FAMILY MEMBERS? ATTACH A SEPARATE SHEET AS NEEDED.

REUNITING

SCHOOL/DAYCARE/WORK	PHONE #	HOW WOULD THEY COMMUNICATE?
_____	_____	_____
_____	_____	_____
_____	_____	_____

EMERGENCY CONTACT OUTSIDE THE COMMUNITY:
NAME: _____   PHONE #   EMAIL   SOCIAL MEDIA
_____   _____   _____   _____

SAFE PLACES

DISASTERS THAT COULD AFFECT US:
_____

IF WE ARE SEPARATED, THESE ARE OUR MEETING PLACES:

NEIGHBORHOOD:	IN COMMUNITY:	OUT OF COMMUNITY:
_____	_____	_____

LEAVING HOME:
POSSIBLE PLACES (PET-FRIENDLY?)

OUR KIT IS READY
(20_____) ○ ○ ○ ○

STAYING HOME:
ROOM NEAR CENTER OF HOME, BASEMENT

OUR KIT IS READY
(20_____) ○ ○ ○ ○

ROUTES

IF WE NEED TO EVACUATE, THESE ARE OUR ROUTES:

ROUTE 1:

ROUTE 2:

ROUTE 3:

Our Emergency Plan - Page 2 of 5

FIGURE 2.2: Family Emergency Plan – HEALTH

(Canvenia, 2023)

our FAMILY EMERGENCY PLAN
HEALTH

Name: _____ Allergies: _____

Conditions: _____

Medications: _____

_____

Name: _____ Allergies: _____

Conditions: _____

Medications: _____

_____

Name: _____ Allergies: _____

Conditions: _____

Medications: _____

_____

Name: _____ Allergies: _____

Conditions: _____

Medications: _____

_____

Pet Name: _____ Allergies: _____

Conditions: _____

Medications: _____

HAVE MORE FAMILY MEMBERS OR INFO? ATTACH A SEPARATE SHEET AS NEEDED.

PROVIDERS & INSURANCE

CONTACT INFO

PRIMARY CARE PROVIDER _____ _____

SPECIALTY DOCTOR _____ _____

PEDIATRIC CARE PROVIDER _____ _____

SPECIALTY DOCTOR _____ _____

DENTIST _____ _____

PEDIATRIC DENTIST _____ _____

VETERINARIAN _____ _____

MEDICAL INSURANCE _____ _____

MEDICAL POLICY # _____

DENTAL INSURANCE _____ _____

DENTAL POLICY # _____

PHARMACY _____ _____

NOTES: _____

Our Emergency Plan - Page 3 of 5

22

FIGURE 2.3: Family Emergency Plan – INSURANCE & SUPPORT

(Canvenia, 2023)

our FAMILY EMERGENCY PLAN
INSURANCE & SUPPORT

FAMILY: _____ ADDRESS: _____

I HAVE DONE THE FOLLOWING

- Recorded possessions in rooms for insurance records, and stored this in a secure place.
- Collected important documents and valuables and secured them in a safe place (safe, other) that can be grabbed or easily retrieved (proof of residency...)

CONTACT INFO

HOMEOWNER/RENTAL INSURANCE		
POLICY #		
OTHER INSURANCE		
POLICY #		
OTHER INSURANCE		
POLICY #		
ELECTRIC COMPANY		
GAS COMPANY		
WATER COMPANY		
TRANSPORTATION		
OTHER		
OTHER		
OTHER		

LOCAL RESOURCES/SUPPORT

WHO	NOTE	CONTACT INFO

Our Emergency Plan - Page 4 of 5

23

Secure Your Documents and Records

"The palest ink is better than the best memory."

– Chinese Proverb

Action Items

- ✓ Video/record possessions in rooms for insurance records, and store in a secure place.
- ✓ Collect your important documents and valuables.
- ✓ Secure important documents in a safe place (e.g. fire-proof safe) that you can retrieve quickly.
- ✓ Call a friend and have a special beverage to celebrate your accomplishments so far.

WHAT DOES IT MEAN TO SECURE DOCUMENTS?

If you find yourself in a disaster, you will need several documents and records during your recovery stage.

- You will need proof of possessions you owned for your insurance company to pay for them or their replacement value. A video of you walking through your house and showing your possessions can help you prove you owned those items.

- You will need "Proof of Residency," which is a utility or similar bill sent to your home address.

- Some documents are sensitive so they should be securely held or backed up so you can access them when you need them. Government documents, such as social security numbers, and any large number of valuables should be secured in something like a fireproof safe or a safety deposit box. If you decide to secure your documents in a fire-proof safe in your home, documents will be safe and easy to grab if you need to evacuate in most scenarios. You may also consider securing copies of sensitive documents electronically, but that is beyond the scope of this book.

However you choose to secure your documents and valuables, use the list below as a checklist to ensure you are being thorough.

REFERENCE LIST: DOCUMENTS

Check off the items you have prepared to be organized, secured, and ready for retrieval in the event of fire or disaster.

1. **Identification Documents:**

   - Birth certificates
   - Passports
   - Social Security cards
   - Driver's licenses
   - Green cards or visas (if applicable)
   - Adoption papers (if applicable)

2. **Financial Documents:**

   - Wills and living wills
   - Trust documents
   - Power-of-attorney documents
   - Deeds and titles for real estate and vehicles
   - Mortgage agreements
   - Insurance policies (life, health, home, auto)
   - Investment account statements
   - Retirement account statements (401k, IRA)
   - Bank account information

3. **Healthcare Documents:**

   - Health insurance cards
   - Medical records
   - Medication lists
   - Living wills or advance directives
   - Durable healthcare power of attorney

4. Legal Documents:

- Marriage certificates
- Divorce decrees
- Custody agreements (if applicable)
- Prenuptial agreements (if applicable)
- Any other legally binding contracts or agreements

5. Property and Asset Documentation:

- Home inventory (photos or videos of valuable possessions)
- Appraisals of valuable items (jewelry, art, antiques)
- Receipts for high-value purchases
- Vehicle titles and registration papers

6. Tax Records:

- Copies of recent tax returns (last 3-5 years)
- Supporting tax documents (W-2s, 1099s, receipts)
- Tax-related correspondence with the IRS or state tax authorities

7. Education Records:

- Diplomas and certificates
- Transcripts
- Education-related financial documents (student loans, scholarships)

8. Legal and Estate Planning Documents:

- Living wills and healthcare proxies
- Guardianship documents (if applicable)
- Trusts and estate planning documents
- Power of attorney documents

9. Important Personal Records:

- Adoption records (if applicable)
- Military service records
- Citizenship or naturalization certificates (if applicable)
- Social Security statements

10. Passwords and Access Information:

- List of important usernames and passwords (stored securely)
- Instructions for accessing digital accounts or assets

11. Family Photos and Videos:

- Copies of digital photos or videos (stored on a flash drive)
- Physical copies of irreplaceable photos or keepsakes

12. Safe Deposit Box Inventory:

- A record of items stored in a bank safe deposit box (if applicable)

You should regularly update and review the contents of your family safe to ensure that it remains current and that you can access important documents quickly in case of emergencies. Keep the safe's combination or key in a secure yet accessible location, known only to trusted individuals, in case you're unable to access it yourself.

Now that you have completed this step, your valuable documents should be fire-safe and accessible, ready for the worst-case scenario. In chapter 4, we'll talk about what to do in case of a fire in your home.

STEP 4

Be Ready for a Fire

"I wish it need not have happened in my time," said Frodo. "So do I," said Gandalf, "and so do all who live to see such times. But that is not for them to decide. All we have to decide is what to do with the time that is given us."

– J.R.R. Tolkien, *The Lord of the Rings*

Action Items

- ✓ Fill out the Family Fire Drill Template.
- ✓ Ensure fire alarms are installed and working.
- ✓ Ensure a fire extinguisher is in an accessible location in your home and you know how to use it.
- ✓ Discuss fire prevention measures with your family.
- ✓ Practice a fire drill with your family.

TOO COMMON TO IGNORE

House fires are a reality in every community. They are sudden and devastating events that demand swift action and a cool head. In this chapter, we will cover crucial aspects of fire safety and preparedness, from preventing fires to knowing how to escape them and effectively use fire extinguishers. This chapter will provide you with the knowledge and skills to protect your home and loved ones from the threat of fires. Your knowledge and plan will protect you as much as an insurance policy helps protect your assets.

FIRE PREVENTION MEASURES

Preventing fires starts with understanding common fire hazards and taking proactive measures to eliminate or reduce them.

Make sure your home has functioning smoke alarms – a minimum of one on every level and one in every bedroom – and test them routinely. The American Red Cross has a program that provides up to three fire alarms for every home, upon request. The alarms have lithium-ion batteries and operate for up to 10 years. Staff will even install them and are able to provide special alarms designed for people who have poor hearing. Wherever you live, regardless of the country, call your local fire department to learn if they can help you.

Avoid overloading electrical outlets. Using extension cords and power strips with multiple devices plugged into them increases your risk for a home fire.

Keep flammable materials away from heat sources. Practice safe cooking habits such as staying near the stove when cooking. If a pan of oil catches on fire, put a cover on it. Without oxygen, the fire will die. And just as you should never leave a stove unattended, never leave candles unattended. Educate your family about fire safety and establish a no-nonsense approach to matches and lighters.

ESCAPING A HOUSE FIRE

Tragically, many people die from home fires every year. In the event of a house fire, a well-rehearsed escape plan can mean the difference between life and death. Designate primary and secondary escape routes from each room, and practice evacuating with your family. Crawling low to the ground to avoid smoke inhalation is essential. Too many people die from smoke inhalation. Also, teach children to touch doors and doorknobs with the back of their hand to check for heat before opening. Teach "Two Ways Out," so your family knows if one exit is blocked by fire or debris, they must use the other exit. The map you make using the template below will help you visualize your exit routes.

USING FIRE EXTINGUISHERS

Fire extinguishers are valuable tools when used correctly and promptly. For general home purposes, a Class A extinguisher is enough. The Pull, Aim, Squeeze, Sweep (P.A.S.S.) technique is a simple method to remember when using a fire extinguisher. However, remember that the safety of you and your family should always be the priority. If the fire becomes uncontrollable, evacuate immediately and call emergency services (Red Cross, 2023, Home Fire Safety).

Fire safety is about more than just knowledge – it's about adopting a proactive mindset and practicing preparedness regularly. By implementing fire prevention measures, rehearsing escape plans, and understanding how to use fire extinguishers, you're creating a shield of preparedness that can ward off the devastating impact of fires. Your commitment to these safety practices ensures that your family is well-equipped to respond effectively and decisively in the face of this potentially life-threatening emergency.

In the next chapter, you'll begin collecting food and other items for your custom Emergency Kit.

FIGURE 4.1: Family Emergency Plan – FIRE DRILL

(Canvenia, 2023)

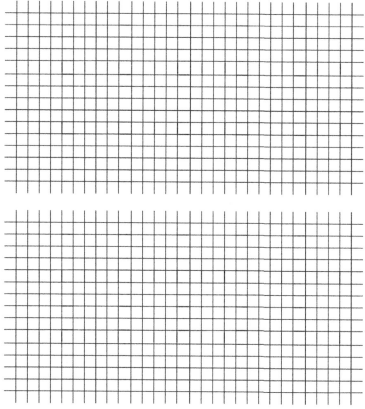

our FAMILY FIRE DRILL

FAMILY: _____   ADDRESS: _____

1. **DRAW A FLOOR PLAN** FOR EACH FLOOR OF YOUR HOUSE
2. **FIND TWO WAYS OUT** OF EVERY ROOM
3. **WHAT ADULT** WILL GET BABIES OR THOSE WHO NEED HELP?
4. LOW PLACES ARE LESS SMOKEY. **STAY LOW.**
5. CLOSED DOORS THAT ARE **HOT DOORS** MUST STAY CLOSED.
6. **PRACTICE** ESCAPING IN LESS THAN 2 MINUTES - EVERYONE
7. MEET AT **OUTSIDE MEETING PLACE**
8. ARE YOUR CLOTHES ON FIRE? **STOP - DROP - ROLL**

Our Emergency Plan - Page 1 of 5

STEP 5

Understand Emergency Kit Basics

"Go to the ant ... consider her ways, and be wise. Without having any chief, officer, or ruler, she prepares her bread in summer and gathers her food in harvest."

– Proverbs 6:6-8

Action Items

In this chapter, you identify what you want. You will collect these items later.

- ✓ Identify foods you want in your emergency kit.
- ✓ Identify your choice of water storage and treatment.
- ✓ Identify how you would prepare food in an emergency.
- ✓ Identify where you will toilet.

THREE KITS, ONE MISSION

Preparedness begins with the right supplies at your fingertips. Your emergency kits are your lifeline when disaster strikes, an insurance policy against uncertainty, and a source of comfort in times of crisis. These kits are designed to sustain you and your loved ones through a wide range of challenges, from natural disasters like hurricanes and earthquakes to unforeseen events like power outages and pandemics.

In this section, we begin a comprehensive exploration of emergency kits, addressing three primary categories:

- **Portable Emergency Kit**: Your "Go-Bag" is a compact, mobile kit filled with the essentials needed for immediate evacuation. It's your ticket to safety when you must leave your home in a hurry.
- **Shelter-in-Place Kit**: This is a comprehensive kit designed to keep you safe and comfortable when you need to stay at home or seek refuge during an emergency. It's a fortress of security within your own four walls.
- **Car Emergency Kit**: This is an often overlooked but vital kit for those moments when you're stranded on the road. It ensures you're prepared for a variety of needs. Of course, if you don't have a vehicle, you can skip this one.

Steps six through eight will cover the details of assembling each of these three kits, helping you identify, choose, pack, and maintain the supplies and quantities you decide are most appropriate for you and your family. You will also learn how to tailor these kits to your unique needs and circumstances, ensuring that your preparedness efforts align with your family's requirements and the specific risks you face.

As you review the information regarding supplies for each kit or category, be aware that there are ways to prepare yourself with minimal effort. There is a methodology that is helpful when approaching the task of building kits. The methodology is Ockham's Razor, a principle used to guide problem-solving and decision-making. Some components of this principle are: "Entities should not be multiplied without necessity" or "The simplest explanation is usually the best one." In other words, if there is a way to accomplish your objectives easier, consider it (Simms, 2023).

One example is to consider how your Go-Bag can be used in your home shelter, so you do not need to duplicate some items that are in your Go-Bag, since you will have it in your home shelter. Another example of simplicity is the availability of pre-made kits such as general disaster kits, tool kits specific to your interests, and food kits that match your tastes. Pre-made kits provide varying amounts of supplies. The Appendix provides you with a range of kits to consider as you purchase supplies. If you choose to purchase one or more, simply check off the items on the Reference Lists as you go along so that you know for certain that you are prepared. There will probably be a small amount of redundancy when using kits, but a "lean machine" is what we're targeting here when it comes to creating your kits.

FOOD

You'll want to stock enough food for anywhere from 3- 30 days. You decide. Your Go-Bag will have three days' worth of food; your Home Kit should have several more days' worth of food. Ten days is recommended for the purposes of quick and fundamental preparedness. You will need foods that have a long shelf life and are high in nutrition. Packages of freeze-dried meals with a shelf-life of 25 years are available, but most require heating water.

Choose foods with high protein, fiber, and nutrient content. In a noteworthy publication by the *Nutrition Journal*, the results of an extensive study highlight the exceptional suitability of nuts and dried fruits for inclusion in emergency kits. The study underscores their remarkable attributes, emphasizing their energy density, outstanding nutritional benefits, universal acceptance across diverse cultures, religious neutrality, prolonged shelf life, minimal storage requirements, ease of handling, no need for prior preparation, and affordability (Wien M, Sabaté J., 2015).

Alongside these energy-rich options, it is important to diversify your food selection for a well-rounded diet that also caters to the specific dietary requirements of your family members. For example, food high in carbohydrates (sugars) can be dangerous for people who have diabetes, so high-protein foods are helpful. Foods that are high in sodium (salt) can be dangerous as we age, as blood pressure is often affected by salt – so low-salt foods are best. Yet arguably equal in importance is incorporating comfort foods into your emergency kits. A chocolate bar may be a welcomed boost in a crisis.

Below is a list of foods for you to consider purchasing for your kits. You can keep some of these items in your Go-Bag. Whether you stay home or leave, your Go-Bag should have three days' worth of nutrition for each person, a minimum of 2,000 calories/day for women and 2,400 calories/day for men (Loma Linda University, 2023). And if you need to shelter in your home, your Go-Bag's supplies will serve you there as well.

REFERENCE LIST: FOODS TO CONSIDER FOR YOUR EMERGENCY KITS

As you review the list below – it is worth repeating – consider adding calorie-dense, easy-to-prepare foods with a long shelf-life. If purchasing cans, consider purchasing cans with pull-tab lids for convenience, or make sure you have a can opener. Everything listed here can be eaten without heating.

- Dried fruits (e.g., raisins, apricots, dates)
- Trail mix or nuts and seeds (e.g., almonds, walnuts, sunflower seeds)
- Canned fruits

- Canned vegetables
- Canned beans
- Canned meats or sealed pouches (e.g., tuna, chicken, salmon)
- Nut butter (e.g., peanut, almond, cashew)
- Canned pudding or fruit cups
- Cereal or granola bars
- Jerky
- Shelf-stable milk (boxed or powdered dairy milk, almond milk, or soy milk)
- Energy bars
- Meal replacement shakes
- Protein powder
- Canned fruit juices
- Baby food: If you have infants or young children, include baby food or formula.
- Comfort foods: Include a few comfort items like chocolate or hard candy for morale.
- Multivitamin supplements: Also consider caffeine supplements if your diet is used to this.

Special Considerations for Health Conditions

HYPERTENSION (HIGH BLOOD PRESSURE)

- Low-sodium (or no-salt added) labels
- Herbs and spices
- Emergency supply of necessary medications (7-day minimum)
- Extra blood pressure monitor, along with extra batteries

DIABETES

- Low-sodium canned legumes and vegetables
- Canned proteins
- Nuts and seeds
- Low-sugar or no-sugar-added nut butters
- Low-sugar or no-sugar-added cereals
- Artificial sweeteners (such as Stevia)
- Shelf-stable unsweetened almond milk or soy milk
- Canned low-sodium broth
- Herbs and spices
- Low-carb canned or pouched meals
- Low-carb meal replacement shakes or bars
- Nutritional drinks for hypoglycemia

- Portable glucose monitoring kit
- Emergency medications
- Low-sugar or no-sugar-added canned fruits
- Extra glucose monitor, as well as testing supplies and extra batteries

WATER

Water is a critical element in any emergency kit. You need to consume enough water in 24 hours to keep your body organs working. Too little water can damage your kidneys, and you need those. Kidney damage can be irreversible. Don't be caught unaware. Here are some important considerations regarding water in your Go-Bag:

Water Quantity: You'll need an adequate supply of water for each person in your household. A general guideline is to store at least one gallon of water per person per day for a minimum of three days. However, consider increasing this amount if you have infants, elderly individuals, or pets. You may not have enough time or ability to carry that much water, or you may run out. For this reason, invest in some options, such as a portable **water filter** for each person in your family and **purification tablets**. When it comes to water storage, too much is always better than the alternative. Consider the natural sources of water in your area, such as streams or rain runoff, and filter the water according to the instructions on whatever product you choose for filtration and purification. If your water has sediment, you should let it settle before using the water. Scoop or pour the clearer water off. You can see product examples in the Appendix. **Note**: If there is a chemical or nuclear accident nearby, you will need to follow advice provided by authorities via your emergency radio. For example, in the case of nuclear fallout, river water and rainwater will be undrinkable.

Bleach can be a useful item to have in a family's emergency shelter, primarily for disinfection and water purification purposes. However, you must understand how to use it safely and effectively. Bleach should only be used when no other water purification method (such as boiling or filtration) is available. Here are some good guidelines:

1. **Water Purification**: Bleach can be used to disinfect water in an emergency, making it safe for drinking. Be sure to use unscented bleach with no additives. Generally, you can use bleach to purify water as follows:

   - Add 8 drops of bleach (about 1/8 of a teaspoon) to one gallon of water.
   - Stir or shake the mixture well.

- Let it stand for 30 minutes.
- The water should have a slight chlorine odor. If it doesn't, repeat the process.

(CDC, 2023, Water Disinfection)

2. **Cleaning and Disinfection**: Bleach can be used to clean and disinfect surfaces in an emergency shelter to maintain hygiene and prevent the spread of diseases. A mixture of bleach and water can be used for cleaning and disinfection, but the exact ratio may vary based on the specific cleaning needs. A common guideline is to mix about 1 tablespoon of bleach with 1 gallon of water for cleaning and disinfecting surfaces. Be sure to follow the instructions on the bleach container and any additional guidance provided by local health authorities.

3. **Storage and Safety**: Proper storage of bleach is vital. Store it in a cool, dry place away from direct sunlight and out of reach of children. Ensure the container is tightly sealed to prevent leakage or evaporation. Always use bleach in a well-ventilated area and avoid inhaling the fumes. Never mix bleach with other cleaning chemicals, as this can produce dangerous fumes.

4. **Labeling and Awareness**: If you use bleach for multiple purposes (e.g., cleaning and water purification), clearly label containers to avoid confusion. Ensure everyone in your family or shelter understands the correct usage and safety precautions associated with bleach.

Having bleach available in an emergency shelter can be valuable for disinfection and water purification, as long as you use it properly, be aware of safety precautions, and store it appropriately to ensure its effectiveness and prevent any adverse effects.

Storage Containers: Food-grade, airtight, and BPA-free containers are easy to find. You can purchase commercially-available water storage containers or thoroughly clean and repurpose used plastic bottles. Make sure the containers are designed for long-term water storage. Our family thoroughly cleans used milk jugs and sports drink bottles (heavy plastic) and fills them with tap water leaving space for the water to expand when frozen. We store these in the freezer when we have extra space. While we wouldn't use these containers for long-term water storage *outside* of the freezer, this approach serves a dual purpose, which is preserving water and keeping a freezer cool in the event of power loss. If you want to use tap water in your water storage plan, be sure to sanitize the containers, fill them to near the top, and rotate (refresh) this water every six months. Our family purchases gallons of water in heavy duty containers at local discount stores, as the shelf life is much longer. Pay attention to any expiration dates on the containers.

Individual Use: Consider including individual-sized water bottles, pouches, or collapsible water containers in your kit, especially in the children's Personal Emergency Kits. These are convenient for personal use and can be easily distributed among family members and refilled. Having their own water in their own kit is empowering for children. Keep in mind that water needs can vary depending on climate, physical activity, and individual health conditions. It's better to have more water than you think you'll need.

Sanitation: Add body wipes to your kit so you can preserve water for hydration. Wipes can help you maintain hygiene and prevent illness during emergencies, while preserving water.

Water for Pets: If you have pets, include water for them in your emergency kit. In fact, a separate "Pet Pack" can help you ensure you have everything your beloved pets need. You can find a Pet Emergency Kit list in the Appendix.

Water is essential for our survival so plan for more than you can imagine you would need.

REFERENCE LIST: WATER SUPPLIES FOR YOUR EMERGENCY KIT

- Water pouches: These pre-packaged, compact pouches have a very long shelf life but can be expensive.
- Plastic bottles: Depending on the thickness of the plastic and shelf life, these have varying value.
- Plastic water bricks: These stack and can be placed in obscure locations, such as under beds.
- Water barrels: Optional siphon pumps can make these more user-friendly.
- Bathtub bladders can be placed in tubs and filled anytime you may anticipate a water shortage.
- Portable water filter: Used to filter water before treatment with purification tablets or bleach.
- Water purification tablets: Used to treat questionable water sources.
- Collapsible water container

HOW WILL YOU PREPARE FOOD?

In times of emergency and limited resources, you'll want to make wise choices for the safety and well-being of yourself and your loved ones. Avoid cooking in confined spaces whenever possible. Open flames or hot appliances can pose serious risks, including fire hazards and the potential for harmful smoke or fumes.

Instead, select foods that can be consumed without the need for heat. This reduces the risks associated with cooking in a confined space. Choose non-perishable, ready-to-eat foods such as canned fruits, protein bars, no-salt nuts, and dried fruits. Choose foods that are nutritionally balanced to keep your energy up during challenging times.

If you want to know more about cooking food or having more interesting meals, you will find solid resources in the section of this book titled, "There's More!" For now, stay focused on fundamentals provided here.

WHEN YOU NEED A RESTROOM

At some point, we all have to go, even in an emergency. No worries! In the event you must hunker down without the luxury of electricity, you can keep a "thunder bucket" in your home shelter. It is a 5-gallon bucket with a tight cover (and an optional seat and privacy curtain).

Next up, you'll begin assembling your Go-Bag.

Create a Portable Emergency Kit (Go-Bag)

"Four things on earth are small, but they are exceedingly wise: the ants are a people not strong, yet they provide their food in the summer."

– Proverbs 30:24-25

Action Items

- ✓ Identify and acquire your portable container.
- ✓ Place food in your Go-Bag.
- ✓ Place water with your Go-Bag.
- ✓ Place clothing and hygiene items in your Go-Bag.
- ✓ Place tools and equipment in your Go-Bag.
- ✓ Consider making a pet disaster kit.

The first emergency kit to create is your Go-Bag. The resources in this kit will also be part of your Shelter-in-Place Plan. Plan for 3 to 7 days of supplies in this kit (and 7 to 14 days in your Shelter-in-Place kit).

Understanding the different types of emergencies empowers you to tailor your preparedness efforts accordingly.

While you may not be able to predict when an emergency will occur, you can certainly prepare for a range of scenarios. The Breakout Box below lists scenarios in which you would want to be able to quickly grab your Go-Bag and leave your home.

Remember that each situation is unique, and when deciding to evacuate, you should listen to official guidance from local authorities and emergency management agencies. Stay informed through reliable sources and follow the instructions provided to ensure the safety of you and your loved ones.

When Should You Take Your Go-Bag?

Below are some examples of emergencies in which you might want to grab your Emergency Kit and leave your home urgently. Keep in mind, you may not have time to safely do this, which is when a car kit can come in extra handy. If you keep your Go-Bag near an exit door, such as a hallway closet, you will be able to grab it quickly, increasing your success in safely escaping with your prepared Go-Bag:

1. **NOTE:** In most circumstances, you can learn from authorities which routes are safe and/or impassable, and changes in weather patterns. If your cell phone is

---

not providing you with updates due to congestion or otherwise, use your weather radio or other means. Information is power when it comes to making decisions that maximize your safety.

2. **Wildfires**

3. **Hurricanes/Tropical Storms**

4. **Floods**: In the case of a tsunami, you may not have time to grab your Go-Bag.

5. **Tornadoes**: Tornadoes can develop quickly and pose a significant threat to homes without a shelter, such as trailer homes, prompting residents to seek shelter and potentially evacuate if the area is impacted.

6. **Earthquakes**: While widely accepted instructions are to "drop, cover and hold on" (Shakeout.org), you may or may not have time to grab your Go-Bag. Always use your judgment.

7. **Chemical Spills/Hazmat Incidents**: Accidents involving hazardous materials can release harmful substances into the air, necessitating evacuations to prevent exposure. Follow guidance to identify areas to avoid, whether evacuating or sheltering-in-place.

8. **Industrial Accidents**: Explosions, fires, or other accidents in industrial areas may require nearby residents to evacuate for safety reasons.

9. **Nuclear Incidents**: While the first action to take after a nuclear incident is to run directly to a basement or inside room, radioactive leaks or other nuclear incidents could require residents to evacuate from affected areas. Always follow advice from authorities (listen with an emergency radio).

10. **Gas Leaks**: Major gas leaks can lead to explosions or other hazards, prompting evacuations to ensure safety.

11. **Biological Threats/Pandemics**: In the case of widespread disease outbreaks or biological threats, evacuation might be necessary to avoid exposure.

12. **Civil Unrest**: During situations of civil unrest or riots, residents may need to evacuate to ensure their safety.

13. **Terrorist Attacks**: In the event of a terrorist attack, evacuation might be required to move away from danger.

14. **Volcanic Eruptions**: Eruptions can result in lava flows, ash clouds, and other hazards that may require evacuation.

15. **Extreme Winter Weather**: Severe winter storms with heavy snowfall and dangerous conditions might require evacuation if homes are at risk of collapse or power outages are prolonged.

16. **Avalanches**: Residents in areas prone to avalanches might need to evacuate if avalanche risk is high.

WHAT GOES INTO A GO-BAG?

As you get ready to assemble your Go-Bag, use the checklist in this chapter to consider what you want to put in your kit. Food and water are always fundamental. When it comes to clothing, err on the side of comfort in the extremes of your local weather. The list will guide you.

Considering duct tape's importance, and with an aim to keep things light, I offer you an ode to duct tape:

Oh, Duct Tape, my close friend, as chaos rages on,
You seal the cracks and holes, my friend, until the break of dawn.
You mend the broken barriers, sealing out the storm,
In makeshift shelter's haven, you keep us safe and warm.
With your strength and versatility, our refuge stands secure,
Oh, Duct Tape, our faithful ally, in adversity we endure.

In all seriousness, duct tape offers enough durability and tough adhesion to make it helpful with holes and weaknesses in many items, including shoes, clothes, backpacks, and most things that leak air or liquid. If you also pack plastic sheeting in your kit, you will be able to make a dry place to sleep almost anywhere. Tents are good, too, but they might take up more space than you want to carry. Duct tape, accompanied with plastic sheeting, will be useful for those who find themselves in a nuclear fallout. You will learn more about this in Step 13.

REFERENCE LIST: ITEMS FOR YOUR GO-BAG

It's time to put together a Go-Bag for your family. Use a large duffle bag that has wheels, or a similar container that is easy to transport, yet large enough to hold all you wish to carry. Below

is a list of items you should consider including in your Go-Bag –
for when you need to leave your home quickly.

- **Documents:** You'll want to have photocopies of things
  that identify you as the resident of a specific property, so
  that you can quickly access resources and insurance.
  You'll also want copies of a recent utility bill and your
  license. Having these items will help you reclaim your
  property faster.

- **Emergency Action Plan:** You created this in Step 2.
  Keep it in your Go-Bag. Pull it out when you conduct your
  drills and review your inventory (twice yearly).

- **Prescription Medications**: Be sure to include a week's
  supply of any necessary prescription medications. Later,
  you will be instructed to add your prescriptions to your
  First-Aid kit, but you may decide to place your
  medications elsewhere in your Go-Bag.

- **Water**: You'll need bottled water or water purification
  tablets to ensure you have clean drinking water.

- **Non-Perishable Food**: Add energy bars, canned goods,
  dried fruits, nuts, or ready-to-eat meals to you kit.

- **Cash**: You'll need small denominations of cash in case
  ATMs are inaccessible.

- **First Aid Kit**: In Step 9 you will add this mini-kit to your Go-Bag, so reserve space in your bag for this.

- **Clothing**: Make sure to add a change of clothes, including sturdy shoes and warm layers. Wool for warmth and cotton for cool is a good guideline to remember.

- **Blankets/Bedding**: Consider adding a compact, lightweight emergency blanket to help each family member keep warm.

- **LED Flashlights:** The LED lantern light can be used for room illumination, individual flashlights, or headlamps, if desired.

- **Weather Alert Radio**: Make sure you include extra batteries or a hand-crank feature.

- **Multi-Tool**: This versatile tool includes pliers, a knife, screwdrivers, and more. Or opt for a little tool kit.

- **Can Opener**

- **Duct Tape**

- **Plastic Sheeting:** Use sheeting to make a dry space/shelter, sealing off outdoor air from entering your shelter, and collecting condensation in hot climates.

- **Whistle**: Can be used to signal for help if needed.

- **Cell Phone Charger**: Portable chargers or a solar charger will help keep your phone powered.

- **Personal Hygiene Items**: Include travel-sized toiletries like toothbrush, toothpaste, soap, and hand sanitizer.

- **Local Map**: It's always helpful to have a physical map of your area in case GPS is unavailable.

- **Notepad and Pen**: Used for jotting down important information or messages.

- **Face Masks**: N-95 are best for most purposes. See the Appendix for an example of masks that can protect you and your children from chemical and radiological disasters.

- **Fire-Starting Supplies:** Include a lighter and tinder or fire starter sticks.

- **Toilet Bucket with Seat and Lid**: Affectionately called "thunder bucket" (deodorizers are available). You will learn more about this option in Step 7.

- **Kitchen-Size Garbage Bags for the Toilet Bucket**

- **Entertainment**: Books, playing cards, or other activities can help pass the time.

- **Baby Supplies**: If you have infants, be sure to pack diapers, formula, bottles, and baby food.

- **Comfort Items**: Consider adding any items that would bring you and your family comfort, such as a teddy bear or chocolate.

- **Pet Supplies**: If you have a pet, include food, water, leash, and any necessary medications. You might want to make a separate disaster kit for them. This can help ensure you do not miss anything essential. See an example check list in the Appendix.

- **Bleach**: Keep this in your home shelter, as it may become helpful to purify water or disinfect items. Always use caution in the placement and storage of this resource, as it is dangerous if used inappropriately.

- **Outdoor Cooking Option**: This book guides you to fundamentally be prepared to handle a disaster without needing to cook food (in case you have no power, you are in a confined space, and unable to go outside or near a vent). You can easily add a small, lightweight, wood-burning camp stove to your Go-Bag. Such stoves use very little wood, can boil water and cook food, and are equipped to charge cell phones and similar devices. It is a good idea to have this packed, along with a lightweight metal pan, but it is not necessary for most short-term emergencies and disasters. Use your discretion, and match your preparedness with the peace of mind you seek.

The items you include in your kit may vary based on your family's needs and the specific type of emergency you might encounter. For example, if a tsunami is impending you will not spend time making an extra trip to grab water.

WHERE WILL YOU PUT YOUR GO-BAG?

People typically place their emergency kits in easily accessible and strategic locations within their houses. Our family puts our Go-Bag on top of a stack of bottled water on the floor in a hallway closet. Our Go-Bag is a large duffle bag with wheels. We each have a backpack as well, so our children can feel empowered and connected to this process of preparedness. It is more personal when we have our own stuff. Our individual backpacks are kept in the same closet, hanging on four hooks, one for each of us. The goal is for everyone in the household to be able to quickly grab the kit and evacuate if needed.

Here are some other common places where people store their emergency kits:

1. **Entryway Closet or Mudroom**: Many households place their emergency kits in an entryway closet or mudroom, especially if it's close to the main exit. This makes it easy to grab the kit on your way out.

2. **Garage or Storage Room**: If you have a garage or a designated storage room, it can be a convenient place to store larger emergency kits or additional supplies.

3. **Under the Bed**: Storing a compact emergency kit under the bed, especially in bedrooms where family members sleep, ensures quick access during the night.

4. **Basement**: If your basement is easily accessible, consider placing an emergency kit there. However, avoid placing it in an area prone to flooding.

5. **Kitchen or Pantry**: In some cases, a kitchen pantry can serve as a good location for storing emergency food supplies. The kit should still be easily portable.

6. **Bedroom Closet**: Storing a smaller emergency kit in a bedroom closet, especially if there is one in each bedroom, allows family members to access kits from different areas of the house.

When it comes to storing your Go-Bag, the most important factor is accessibility. Your emergency kit should be easy to reach, even in the dark or during high-stress situations. Remember to store your valuable documents (including any significant amount of cash, for example) in a safe or other secure place so that you can easily get to it when you need to evacuate. Exceptions to safely grabbing your kits and/or secured documents include home fires and earthquakes. Always use your judgment based on the situation at hand.

WHEN TO EVACUATE

When you're facing the need to leave your home because of a threat, it's a wise idea to stay on top of alerts and listen to the radio for shelter info. Send a text to your friends or family who might have a safe place for you. These threats could be hurricanes, floods, wildfires, or even emergencies like chemical spills or power outages. As part of your emergency plan, you have already identified possible meeting places and shelters, including pet-friendly hotels.

Now that you have your Go-Bag ready, next up you'll work on the assembly of your Shelter-at-Home kit. Be sure to celebrate all the progress you've made so far.

Create a Shelter-in-Place Kit

"And take with you every kind of food that is eaten, and store it up. It shall serve as food for you and for them."

– Genesis 6:21 (ESV)

Action Items

- ✓ Identify and make a shelter space in your home.
- ✓ Place food in a storage container, shelf, or area.
- ✓ Place water in your shelter.
- ✓ Have a tote dedicated to additional bedding and clothing.
- ✓ Place a more-robust hygiene kit in your shelter space (for toileting, bathing, etc.).

While having a Go-Bag is crucial, it is equally important to prepare for scenarios in which you need to stay in your home for an extended period. A Shelter-in-Place kit ensures that you have the supplies necessary to weather a crisis from the comfort of your own home. The Red Cross recommends you have enough supplies in your home shelter to allow you to be independent for two weeks (Red Cross, 2023). Try to make this a goal. In this chapter, we'll explore the components of a Shelter-in-Place kit, allowing you to transform your home into a safe haven during emergencies.

IDENTIFY A SPACE IN YOUR HOME FOR AN EMERGENCY SHELTER

Without a doubt, civil unrest, war, and nuclear disasters present the worst-case-scenario approach to prepping. Because this book is focused on empowering you for most situations, your home shelter should be toward the center of your building and on a lower level. Keep this ideal location in mind as you consider where you might shelter-in-place.

HOW TO EASILY MANAGE YOUR EMERGENCY SUPPLIES

Totes make it easy to isolate your kit from your other supplies, allowing you to label expiration dates on totes, which saves you time in managing the inventory. Include canned goods, dry fruits, nuts, and high-energy snacks, as listed earlier. Our family uses three totes: one for items that have a shelf life over five years, one for items that have a shelf life over 2 years, and one for items that expire in less than 2 years. Step 11 will guide you to incorporate camping-style drills twice yearly. During these drills, you will use some supplies, become familiar with them, and rotate items based on expiration dates.

WATER SOURCES IN YOUR HOME

When sheltering at home, you should have more water stored to sustain your family. Consider water purification methods in case water becomes compromised or you need to seek an external source. In addition to the ways of storing and treating water already discussed, you may have the added benefit of having access to your water heater.

WATER CAN BE PRESERVED IN YOUR PIPES AND WATER HEATER

In an emergency such as any power outage, earthquake, hurricane/tropical storm, or nuclear disaster, you can shut off the water coming from your municipality or well to both keep the water in your house and keep chemicals or pollutants from entering your home through the water. For whatever reason you want to trap the water in your home, you can potentially add several days' water supply for your family. Hot water heaters alone usually hold between 30 and 50 gallons of water.

Here are some tips on accessing the water in your water heater:

1. If you have access to the valve that opens and closes the water pipe entering your home, close it as soon as you lose power or in anticipation of a reason to need to preserve your water.

2. If you do not have access to the valve, but you DO have access to your hot water heater, close the water-intake valve at the top of the unit. This will contain the water. Be certain you have turned off the gas, and be sure not to turn the electricity back on if the tank is not able to refill, or the water valve is off.

3. You can access the water by placing a clean container under the faucet that is at the base of the unit.

4. You should treat the water by boiling, chlorination, or filtration, as discussed earlier.

(County of Alameda, California, 2023, Emergency Water)

ANSWERING NATURE'S CALL (TOILETING)

If you find yourself sheltering in your home without power or running water, you will also want to have a plan for your restroom needs. Affectionately called a "thunder bucket," a 5-gallon pail with a tight-sealing cover can serve as your makeshift emergency toilet. It is a practical solution for maintaining hygiene and sanitation during an emergency or disaster situation. Here's how you can set up such a system:

Materials Needed:

1. **5-Gallon Pail with Lid:** A pail with a tight-sealing lid will contain odors and prevent spills.

2. **Toilet Seat or Lid:** While not absolutely necessary, attaching a toilet seat or lid to the pail can make it more comfortable to use. These are specially made to snap on and seal but can be difficult to attach.

3. **Plastic Bags:** Use heavy-duty, leak-proof plastic bags designed for waste disposal. These bags line the inside of the pail to contain waste.

4. **Toilet Paper or Wet Wipes**

5. **Hand Sanitizing Wipes**

SETUP AND USE OF THE THUNDER BUCKET:

Place a plastic bag inside the pail, ensuring it covers the entire interior. Leave some of the bag hanging over the edge of the pail. When nature calls, sit on the pail as you would on a regular toilet. Kits often include a privacy curtain. To control odors, you can sprinkle a small amount of deodorant crystals or baking soda into the bag before using it. After one or a few uses, tie a knot in the bag to seal it and contain the waste securely. You can then place the sealed bag in another sturdy plastic bag or a designated container for double containment. Follow local regulations for waste disposal.

It is possible to maintain hygiene and sanitation during an emergency. You can prevent the spread of disease and maintain your overall well-being. Having a dedicated space for sanitation and a well-thought-out plan for waste disposal, along with supplies like toilet paper, hand wipes, and deodorizers, can help you and your family maintain good hygiene even when regular facilities are not available.

SCENARIOS OF SHELTERING-IN-PLACE

Knowing when to shelter-in-place requires monitoring emergency alerts and understanding the dangers involved. Situations like chemical spills, air pollution, or extreme weather can warrant this response. Your Shelter-in-Place kit should be well-stocked. With some simple planning, you can be prepared to remain indoors for 7- 14 days – or until given the all-clear. Keep your emergency weather radio handy!

Because cold weather can present some unique challenges, below are some additional considerations for readers who live in a tundra.

FREEZING TEMPERATURES IN A POWER OUTAGE

A prolonged power outage in a sub-zero climate can be a challenging and potentially life-threatening situation. Here are some considerations:

1. Keep doors closed: This may seem like common sense, but if you have family members, you know vigilance is a challenging thing to maintain. And freezing temperatures outside requires vigilance.

2. If you have the means to heat with propane, kerosene, or firewood, you should have a battery-powered carbon monoxide alarm in your emergency kit. Err on the side of caution.

3. Clothing needs to be in layers and abundant. "Wool, silk, or polypropylene will hold more body heat than cotton" (CDC, 2023, Stay Safe).

4. Regarding your home, keep cold things closed and warm things open (EPA, 2023).

    a. Try to keep your freezer and refrigerator closed.
    b. Open blinds on windows that have sunlight beaming in.
    c. Close blinds and curtains everywhere there is no sunlight warming the space.

    d. Plastic sheeting and duct tape can seal leaks.

5. Communication can be maintained: Cell phone batteries may die, so plan to have a backup means for charging devices. Hand-crank emergency radios often have a port to charge your phone or other device while also providing you with updates from authorities. Shelters may become available, so you'll want to listen for that information. Another means for charging your cell phone is the lightweight, wood-burning cook stove (for outdoor use only). You can see this in the Appendix, under Resources.

6. Medical needs: Individuals with medical conditions that rely on powered medical equipment should consider alternative power sources and options or contact healthcare providers for guidance.

7. Available Shelters: If you choose to go to one, keep in mind the needs of your home. As temperatures drop, there is a risk water pipes freeze and subsequently burst. If you can minimize the time entry-doors are open, you can reduce the risk of property damage and prolonged water outage (occurs when pipes burst due to expanding/freezing water). Open bathroom and kitchen cabinet doors to allow air to circulate and equalize (Red Cross, 2023, Frozen Pipes).

A family's decision to shelter at home is usually based on the nature of the emergency and on communication from authorities. Next, we'll consider roadside emergencies, as preparedness can hedge your bets in favor of success.

Create a Car Emergency Kit

"Cars are the sculptures of our everyday lives."

– Chris Bangle

Action Items

- ✓ Ensure your vehicle maintenance is up to date.
- ✓ Identify container for your vehicle's emergency kit.
- ✓ Place your tools and safety equipment in your kit.
- ✓ Add copies of your emergency contacts, maps, routes.
- ✓ Include food and water in your kit.
- ✓ Place clothes and hygiene items in your kit.

Your vehicle can serve as both a mode of transportation and a temporary shelter during emergencies. Just as you've prepared your home and Go-Bag, it's a good idea to extend your readiness to your vehicle, if you have one. Your Car Kit, does not need to duplicate your Go-Bag. You should have 3 solid days of supplies in your Go-Bag when you need to evacuate your home. But you will benefit from pretending your vehicle breaks down in an unpleasant place. In this section, you'll assemble your car kit. Be aware that there are pre-made kits available if you prefer to cut corners. You can check off the items below that are included in any kit you buy or any item you add.

VEHICLE MAINTENANCE

Before you begin the task of kit creation, consider your vehicle's maintenance needs. Take a lesson from Isabel the Bunjitsu Bunny, the wise student of conflict-avoidance in a children's story written by John Himmelman. In the endearing series, she uses her martial arts skills not to fight but to avoid or peacefully resolve conflicts and challenges she encounters. Applying this principle to having a robust emergency kit in your vehicle, you should first address your vehicle's preparedness to avoid conflict by making sure it's up to date on maintenance. Bunjitsu Bunny was fully prepared for conflict, but she avoided it wherever possible.

While this section will help you make a car kit, some emergencies can be avoided altogether if you stick to a maintenance plan, as recommended by your vehicle's manufacturer. It includes specific tasks at certain mileage intervals. Special considerations need to be made for extreme temperatures. Ask your mechanic any questions you have. See the BREAKOUT box below for freezing temperatures.

YOUR CAR KIT

Your Car Kit is an extension of your overall preparedness efforts. Whether you're facing a sudden breakdown, unexpected weather conditions, or any other challenges on the road, the items in your kit can provide you comfort, safety, and peace of mind. Below is a list of items for you to consider collecting. Remember kits are available if you want to simplify the process. Consider the unique challenges your region presents – for instance, desert areas may require additional water and sun protection items. Regularly check and update your kit's contents to ensure that everything is in good working condition. By having a well-stocked vehicle emergency kit, you're not only safeguarding your journey but also empowering yourself to navigate unexpected situations with confidence.

REFERENCE LIST: ITEMS TO CONSIDER FOR YOUR CAR EMERGENCY KIT

- **Reflective Triangles or Road Flares:** Enhance visibility and safety if your car breaks down on the road.

- **Duct Tape:** Useful for taping flares and triangles to high places.

- **Spare Tire & Tools or Tire Repair Kit:** Research indicates a spare tire is both a cheaper and more dependable solution for flat tires (AAA, 2015). Many newer vehicles are not equipped with a spare tire.

- **First Aid Kit:** Includes bandages, antiseptic wipes, adhesive tape, scissors, tweezers, pain relievers, and any necessary personal medications.

- **Blankets or Sleeping Bags:** These can provide warmth in case of breakdowns or getting stranded.

- **Flashlight and Extra Batteries:** A reliable flashlight is a must for nighttime emergencies.

- **Jumper Cables:** Highly recommended, these can save you and others time and money.

- **Basic Tools:** Screwdrivers, pliers, adjustable wrench, and a Swiss army knife or a similar tool.

- **Tire Pressure Gauge:** Regularly check and maintain proper tire pressure.

- **Non-Perishable Snacks:** Granola bars, nuts, and dried fruits can provide sustenance during extended waits.

- **Bottled Water:** Carry several bottles for hydration. See Cold Weather Considerations below.

- **Fire Extinguisher:** A small, multi-purpose fire extinguisher can be invaluable in case of a car fire.

- **Tow Strap or Chain:** In case your car needs to be towed.

- **Rain Poncho or Jacket**

- **Warm Clothing:** Keep extra gloves, hats, and socks in case you need them.

- **Car Manual:** Consult your car's manual for specific instructions in case of breakdowns.

- **Maps:** A physical map of your local area can be handy if your GPS or phone is not working.

- **Paper and Pen:** Useful for leaving notes or jotting down information.

- **Portable Phone Charger:** Keep your phone charged to call for help or assistance.

- **Emergency Whistle:** Can be used to signal for help.

- **Car Escape Tool:** A tool designed to break glass and cut seatbelts, useful in case of an accident.

- **Cash:** Carry some small bills in case you need to pay for services.

- **Traction Aids:** If you live in an area with snow and ice, consider sand, cat litter, or traction mats to help get your car unstuck.

- **Gloves and Rags:** For handling tools, changing tires, and staying clean.

- **Important Documents:** Keep copies of your registration and insurance information in a waterproof bag.

Remember to periodically check and update the items in your car emergency kit to ensure they are in good condition and up to date. Always tailor your kit to your specific needs and regional climate conditions.

COLD WEATHER PRECAUTIONS

If you live in a cold climate, you will want to take a few more precautions. If you get stuck in snow and do not have immediate help, turn on your warning lights. If you have a strobe or flare light, place it near the top of your vehicle; tape it with duct tape if you need to. Here are some guidelines to remember:

- Stay off the roads when conditions are dangerous.

- Always keep your gas tank over half full.
- Replace worn tires and check air pressure of tires.
- Car maintenance needs to include antifreeze check.
- If stranded, shovel snow away from your exhaust pipe to protect against carbon monoxide poisoning can result.
- Run the engine for about 10 minutes every hour.

You should have winter supplies in your Car Kit that include the following:

- Ice scraper and snow brush
- Snow shovel
- Hand warmers
- Sand or kitty litter can provide traction under tires if stuck in snow or on ice
- Extra warm clothing (hats, gloves, socks, winter coats, warm snow boots)
- Wool blankets or sleeping bags
- Carbon monoxide detector

(CDC, 2023, #PrepYourHealth to Drive During Winter)

Now that your Car Kit is ready, next up, it's time to assemble a comprehensive First Aid Kit.

Create a First Aid Kit

*"The best emergency kit is the one
you never have to use."*

– Anonymous

Action Items

- ✓ Make a medication list for each family member (drug name, strength, dose, frequency).
- ✓ Pack seven days doses minimum (remember to rotate).
- ✓ Collect general supplies and package them OR buy a prepackaged kit.
- ✓ Add the completed First Aid Kit to your Go-Bag.

Scenario of a Family's Use of First Aid in their Emergency Shelter

John and Sarah Smith and their two children, Emma and Liam, found themselves in a challenging situation one stormy night. A powerful hurricane had made landfall in their coastal town, causing widespread damage and power outages. With no electricity and limited access to medical facilities due to flooding and road closures, the Smiths were forced to rely on their well-stocked first-aid kit and basic emergency care skills they had learned from a general emergency care guide.

As the storm raged outside, their home sustained minor damage, causing a glass shard to cut Emma's arm when a window shattered. The family had prepared their home as an emergency shelter, with supplies like bottled water, non-perishable food, flashlights, and a battery-operated radio. They also had a well-stocked first-aid kit on hand.

HOW THEIR KIT AND SKILLS PROVED BENEFICIAL:

1. Immediate Response:

- Sarah, who had read the emergency care guide, quickly assessed Emma's injury. Sarah used gloves from the first-aid kit to prevent infection and gently cleaned the wound with antiseptic wipes to remove any debris.
- John grabbed the clean gauze pads, adhesive bandages, and medical tape from the kit. He applied pressure to the wound to stop the bleeding and secured the bandage in place.
- Knowing basic first-aid, Sarah elevated Emma's injured arm to reduce swelling.

2. Communication:

- While Sarah attended to Emma's wound, John used the battery-operated radio to stay updated on local emergency broadcasts and make sure they were aware of any evacuation orders or additional storm warnings.

3. Pain Management:

- The first-aid kit contained over-the-counter pain relievers, which they gave to Emma to help manage her pain while waiting for a chance to take her seen by a medical provider.

4. Monitoring and Comfort:

- Liam, their older child, had learned how to take a person's vital signs, such as temperature and pulse, from the emergency care guide. He periodically checked Emma's vital signs and reported them to his parents, helping to monitor her condition.
- Sarah also comforted Emma, reassuring her and keeping her calm during the stressful situation.

5. Long-Term Care:

- With no immediate access to medical facilities, the Smiths continued to clean and dress Emma's wound regularly over the next few days, using supplies from their well-stocked first-aid kit.

- John and Sarah kept an eye on Emma's wound for any signs of infection.

As the storm gradually subsided, emergency services reached the Smith's neighborhood. Thanks to their well-prepared emergency shelter and the basic emergency care skills they had learned, the Smith family was able to provide immediate and essential care to Emma. Their well-stocked first-aid kit and knowledge of emergency care provided Emma safety and comfort during the critical period when professional medical assistance was not available.

ESSENTIAL FIRST AID SUPPLIES

Ready to build your own First Aid Kit? Below, you'll find a list of items categorized by Personal, General, and Special Items. If you decide to purchase a ready-to-go kit, check off the items in the "General" category below that are in your kit. Add any of your personal and special supplies and your kit will be complete.

Prescribed medicine is best kept where you will remember it is and it is readily available. I try to keep all medical things together so that I know exactly where to go when I need it. You will find your preference as you move along on this path of preparedness.

REFERENCE LIST: SUPPLIES FOR YOUR FIRST AID KIT

First Aid Bag or Container: Start by finding a durable, waterproof container to contain your first aid supplies.

Personal:

- **Prescription Medications**: If you or your family members require prescription medications, keep an emergency supply of 7 days minimum, if possible.
- **Your Emergency Plan:** The Plan you completed (including Personal Health Records and Emergency Numbers) can be kept here or in another place in your Go-Bag.
- **Eyeglasses or Contact Lenses**: Spare glasses or contacts and cleaning solution, if needed. Include a hard case for glasses or protective containers for contact lenses.

General:

- **Foot Care**: Pack blister prevention items, such as moleskin or blister pads, to take care of your feet during extended walks.

- **Adhesive Bandages**: Include various sizes of adhesive bandages for covering minor cuts and abrasions.

- **Sterile Gauze Pads**: Used for wound dressing and to stop bleeding from larger wounds.

- **Antiseptic Wipes**: These are handy for cleaning wounds and preventing infection.

- **Antibacterial Ointment**: Helps prevent infection in minor cuts and scrapes.

- **Scissors and Tweezers**: These tools are useful for cutting tape, clothing, or removing splinters.

- **Cotton Balls or Swabs**: For cleaning and applying medications.

- **Medical Tape**: Used for securing bandages and dressings in place.

- **Elastic Bandage (Ace Bandage)**: Provides support for sprains, strains, and injuries.

- **Disposable Gloves**: Protect yourself and others when administering first aid.

- **Thermometer**: For monitoring body temperature, especially during illness.

- **Pain Relievers**: Include over-the-counter pain relievers, like acetaminophen or ibuprofen.

- **Allergy Medication**: Antihistamines can help manage allergic reactions.

- **Eyewash or Saline Solution**: For rinsing eyes if exposed to irritants.
- **Instant Cold Packs**: Provide relief for sprains, strains, and swelling.
- **CPR Mask**: If you are trained in CPR, a mask can protect you while providing rescue breaths.
- **Emergency Blankets**: Reflective emergency blankets help retain body heat. Have one for each family member.
- **Burn Cream or Gel**: For treating minor burns.
- **Personal Protective Equipment (PPE):** N95 masks, safety goggles, and disposable gloves for safety during hazardous conditions.
- **First Aid Manual**: A guide for administering first aid.

Special Items:

- **Children and Infants**: If you have young children or infants, include child-specific first aid supplies, such as pediatric medications and baby-sized bandages.
- **Allergies and Medical Conditions**: Tailor your first aid kit to accommodate specific allergies and medical conditions within your family. You may want to include EpiPens or asthma inhalers.

- **Rotating supplies:** Twice yearly, check and replenish the contents, ensuring that items have not expired and are in good condition. See Step 11 for more on this.
- **Low-Cost Community Courses:** Consider taking a basic first aid and CPR course (such as one provided by the Red Cross) to equip yourself with the skills needed to provide effective assistance during emergencies.

Scenario of a Family's Evacuation and the Importance of Their First-Aid Kit

As the hurricane continued to unleash its fury on Harborville, the Smith family monitored the situation closely through their battery-operated radio. Emergency broadcasts indicated that the storm surge was rising rapidly, posing a serious threat to their coastal community. With their home now at risk of flooding, they knew they had to make a difficult decision: evacuate to a safer location.

The Smiths had a well-thought-out evacuation plan in place, including a designated meeting point and a Go-Bag with essential supplies. They also carried their first-aid kit to ensure their safety during the evacuation.

As they hurriedly packed their bags, they faced another stressful situation. While securing their belongings, Sarah accidentally slipped on a wet floor and twisted her ankle. The pain was immediate, and she found it difficult to put weight on her injured leg.

Their first-aid kit, which they had diligently maintained and restocked, proved to be indispensable once again. Here's how it played an important role:

1. Immediate First Aid:

- John, with his knowledge of basic first-aid techniques from the emergency care guide, quickly assessed Sarah's injury.
- He retrieved the instant cold pack from the first-aid kit to reduce swelling and alleviate some of her pain.
- With Liam's assistance, Sarah gently applied an elastic bandage from the kit to stabilize her ankle, providing support during their evacuation.

2. Pain Management:

- Inside the kit, they found the over-the-counter pain relievers, which Sarah took to help manage her pain and discomfort, allowing her to keep moving.

3. Continued Care:

- As they left their home and joined their neighbors in the evacuation process, the Smiths kept the first-aid kit within reach in case they needed additional supplies during their journey.
- They also had adhesive bandages and antiseptic wipes readily available in case of any minor injuries or wounds sustained during the evacuation.

Thanks to their well-stocked first-aid kit and the knowledge they had gained from the emergency care guide, the Smith family could provide immediate care to Sarah's injured ankle, even while evacuating their home. In times of crisis, when professional medical help might be far away or delayed, having a properly equipped first-aid kit and the skills to use it effectively can make a significant difference in the safety and well-being of loved ones during an evacuation. Even children can feel empowered by knowing what is available for them in the event they should need something from the kit.

In the next step, we'll talk about how to get your children involved in the prepping process.

Getting Children Involved

"You have brains in your head. You have feet in your shoes. You can steer yourself any direction you choose."

– Dr. Seuss, *Oh, the Places You'll Go!*

Action Items

- ✓ If you do not have children, you may skip this step.
- ✓ Provide the Template for each child to review.
- ✓ Provide a small backpack or bag for each child.
- ✓ Encourage independence.

CONTAINERS AND TEMPLATES

As parents, we want our children to feel empowered through this lifelong process of being prepared. Giving children their own emergency backpacks can encourage honest and adventurous discussions.

Templates 10.1 and 10.2 are tools to help your **young child** feel connected to you and your mission of being prepared.

Encourage them to place their completed Plan in their emergency backpack.

Templates 10.3 and 10.4 are tools to help your **older child or teen** feel connected to you and your mission of being prepared. Encourage them to place their completed Plan in their emergency backpack.

HELPING YOUNG CHILDREN DEVELOP PREPPING SKILLS AND COURAGE

You will notice a section on Template 10.1 to list skills. Encourage play/acting to practice skills. Here are some examples of ways children can practice their strengths and skills.

1. **Teddy Bear First Aid**: Your child's favorite stuffed animal, Teddy, has a rip. He "treats" the injury by using a small bandage (from his toy doctor kit) and gently stitches up the teddy's tear, demonstrating basic first-aid skills.

2. **Stuffed Animal Earthquake Drill**: Your child practices what to do during an "earthquake drill" with her stuffed animals. She demonstrates by dropping to the ground, taking cover under a table, and holding onto her stuffed animals for safety.

3. **Stuffed Animal "Phone Call"**: Your child and his stuffed animals pretend to make an emergency "phone call" to a toy phone. He practices speaking clearly and providing his name and address as if calling for help.

4. **Stuffed Animal Weather Report**: Your child uses her toy weather station to give a weather report to her stuffed animals. She discusses what to do in various weather emergencies, like putting on a raincoat during pretend rain.

These scenarios can help your children develop problem-solving skills, foster their imaginations, and introduce basic safety concepts in a child-friendly way. Parents and caregivers can encourage such imaginative play and reinforce important safety lessons through these activities.

FIGURE 10.1: Child's Emergency Kit Plan

(Canvenia, 2023)

my PERSONAL EMERGENCY KIT

MY FAMILY NAME: _____ OUR ADDRESS: _____

DATE: _____

THIS IS ME

CONTACT INFO

I KNOW HOW
THESE ARE MY SKILLS

1	
2	
3	
4	

MY KIT IS PACKED!

IMPORTANT ITEMS
ARE PACKED!

Food ◯
Water ◯
One Change of Clothes ◯
Tooth Brush ◯
Body Wipes ◯
Toy ◯
Game ◯
Book ◯
Paper & Pen ◯
This Page ◯

FIGURE 10.2: Child's Emergency Kit Checklist

(Canvenia, 2023)

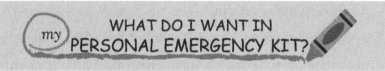

WHAT DO I WANT IN my PERSONAL EMERGENCY KIT?

_____ A Bottle of Water
_____ Granola Bar
_____ Clothing (one change)
_____ Blanket (light weight)
_____ LED Flashlight

Body Wipes _____
Toothbrush _____
Coins / Money _____
Bandaids _____
Face Mask _____
Paper and Pen or Crayon _____
Books, Playing Cards, Toys. _____

SPECIAL REQUESTS

_____
_____
_____
_____

HELPING CHILDREN AGES 8 TO 12 DEVELOP PREPPING SKILLS AND COURAGE

Children between the ages of 8 and 12 can learn and develop a range of valuable skills related to safety, self-reliance, and emergency preparedness. Here are some skills that children in this age group may know or want to learn:

- **Basic First Aid**: They can learn how to clean and dress minor wounds, apply bandages, and understand when and how to call for help in more serious situations.

- **CPR and AED**: Children can begin to learn basic cardiopulmonary resuscitation (CPR) techniques.

- **Fire Safety**: They should understand how to use a fire extinguisher, how to stop, drop, and roll in case of clothing fire, and how to create and practice a fire escape plan.

- **Severe Weather Preparedness**: They can learn about weather-related safety, including what to do during storms, tornadoes, hurricanes, or wildfires.

- **Basic Navigation**: They can learn to read and use maps, compasses, or navigation apps to avoid getting lost when hiking or in unfamiliar places.

These skills not only enhance a child's safety, but also promote independence and self-confidence. Teach these skills gradually, reinforce them through practice, and tailor the lessons to the child's individual maturity and capabilities.

HELPING TEENS DEVELOP PREPPING SKILLS AND COURAGE

Teenagers also gain confidence by realizing their skills are valuable in emergency situations. The following skills encompass a wide range of safety, first aid, communication, and problem-solving abilities, empowering teenagers to respond effectively when faced with various unexpected and challenging circumstances. By encouraging the development of these skills, you can significantly enhance your teens preparedness, self-reliance, and confidence in times of crisis.

- **First Aid and CPR**: Basic knowledge of first aid and CPR can be used to address injuries and medical emergencies.

- **Car Maintenance**: Basic car maintenance skills help to handle breakdowns and car-related emergencies.

- **Heimlich Maneuver**: The ability to perform the Heimlich maneuver can save the life of someone choking on an object.

- **Fire Safety**: Knowledge of fire safety protocols, including the use of fire extinguishers and evacuation procedures is useful for teens.

- **Allergic Reaction Response**: Ability to recognize and address severe allergic reactions, including how to use an epinephrine auto-injectors.

- **Wildlife Awareness**: Awareness of how to handle wildlife encounters and understanding various responses to different animals.

- **Outdoor Survival Skills**: Knowledge of camping and survival skills, including shelter-building, fire-making, and foraging.

- **Emergency Preparedness**: Preparedness for various emergencies, including natural disasters, with the ability to implement emergency plans.

- **Communication**: Effective communication skills to relay information and stay calm during emergency situations.

- **Self-Defense Basics**: Basic self-defense techniques for personal safety in potentially dangerous situations.

- **Navigation and Map Reading**: Ability to use maps, compasses, and digital navigation tools for orientation and direction-finding.

- **Problem-Solving and Decision-Making**: Critical thinking and decision-making skills to respond appropriately in emergencies.

Teaching teenagers these skills not only enhances their ability to respond to emergencies but also fosters self-confidence, independence, and a sense of responsibility. Parents play an important role in imparting these life-saving skills and reinforcing them through practice and training.

CHALLENGE: Ask your teen if there is something they would like to learn. There are many classes, both online and in person, that can empower your teenager to learn useful life skills.

In the next step, I'll show you how to conduct practice drills to benefit you and your family.

FIGURE 10.3: Teen's Emergency Kit Plan

(Canvenia, 2023)

Teen
my PERSONAL EMERGENCY KIT

MY FAMILY NAME: _____   OUR ADDRESS: _____

DATE: _____

ME: _____

IMPORTANT
CONTACTS

MY SKILLS

_____

_____

_____

_____

_____

_____

_____

MY KIT IS PACKED

Food ◯

Water ◯

Clothes ◯

Tooth Brush, Paste, Floss ◯

Body Wipes ◯

Flashlight ◯

Tools ◯

Book, Games ◯

Paper & Pen ◯

This Page ◯

◯

IMPORTANT ITEMS
ARE PACKED!

FIGURE 10.4: Teen's Go-Bag Shopping List

(Canvenia, 2023)

Teen
PERSONAL EMERGENCY KIT CHECKLIST

_____ Water
_____ Protein Bars or
_____ Clothes
_____ Sleeping Bag or
_____ LED Flashlight
_____ Body Wipes
_____ Toothbrush, Toothpaste & Floss
_____ Money
_____ Multipurpose Tool
_____ Face Mask
_____ Meal Kit/Bowl & Utensil
_____ Books, Entertainment

_____ _____
_____ _____
_____ _____
_____ _____
_____ _____
_____ _____
_____ _____

NOTES

_____
_____
_____
_____
_____
_____

Drills: Pretending Builds Psychological Preparedness

"Drills and skills pay the bills."

– Anonymous

Action Items

- ✓ Plan for an emergency drill.
- ✓ Add it to your calendar.
- ✓ Discuss the drill with your family.

CONFIDENCE COMES WITH PRACTICE

In our family, every day is an adventure. Daily we face challenges and build bonds. Emergency preparedness is one more opportunity to build those bonds. By practicing drills and making the maintenance of our kits a seasonal tradition, it becomes an adventure that empowers us as a familial unit. Our family goes through this process, and we learn together. We find out what we hate, what we can tolerate, and what we want to change in our plans and kits.

The same sources I have referenced throughout this book all advise you to refresh your kits twice yearly to ensure everything is functional and safe, but this does not have to be a boring chore. Instead, it can be a time of bonding, a tradition, and an opportunity to have conversations you normally wouldn't have. It's also the perfect time to conduct practice drills. This chapter will outline scenarios of various kinds of drills with your family.

WHAT IS THE PURPOSE OF A DRILL?

The main purpose of a drill is to find things you like and don't like about your planning and adjust those plans for next time. Also, drills are a great time to go through each of your emergency kits to replace items that need to be replaced due to expiration dates.

WHAT DO YOU NEED FOR A DRILL?

Do you need to prepare anything? Absolutely not. This is a test. Don't pack any additional supplies. Use only the kits and adjust them after you've had your drill and reflected on what you want to improve the next time.

TALKING ABOUT THE UPCOMING DISASTER DRILL

It's April and your family has planned this mock-disaster much as you would a vacation. The day for the drill comes, and you pretend there is severe weather. You live in a region prone to severe weather, including occasional power outages and natural disasters. As part of your emergency preparedness plan, you have a well-stocked emergency shelter in your basement or a designated safe area within your home. Your shelter includes your essential supplies as addressed in this book.

If you have completed your Emergency Plan, your Go-Bag, and your Shelter-in-Place Kit, then you are ready to practice the drill.

Use the examples below to discuss with your family (or roommates) your upcoming drill. A drill is recommended to be done every six months, around April and November.

Example Drill for a Home Fire

1. On the designated day, discuss with your family the two exits from every room.
2. As soon as a fire alarm sounds, set your timer for two minutes and see if everyone can get out quickly.
3. Remind family members to craw because smoke rises and feel doors before opening them.
4. Choose an outdoor landmark in the yard where your whole family can convene.

5. Is there anyone who needs help (baby, toddler, or elderly person)? Which adult will be responsible to help that person? What about pets?

6. With a fire, do not take the time to grab your Go-Bag unless it is in the same room as you. Aim to get everyone out of the house in under two minutes.

Example Drill for Sheltering-in-Place (Staying Home)

1. On the designated day, turn off the main power to your home or turn off all lights and powered devices to simulate a power outage. Do NOT turn off gas.

2. Gather all family members and pets and go to the shelter space in your home with flashlights in hand.

3. Use your emergency supplies to prepare a meal in your shelter space.

4. Practice personal hygiene using the Shelter-in-Place kit.

5. Eat your meal by lantern (LED), listening to the weather radio.

6. Review emergency situations (Infographics) in this book, *Disaster Ready.*

7. Play cards or some other form of entertainment.

8. Set up your portable potty if you wish.

9. Roll out your bedding and sleep.

10. In the morning, eat and drink from your kit.

11. Once again, practice personal hygiene using the kit.

12. After the drill, discuss what went well and what you could improve. Take notes of any items in your emergency kit that need replenishing or updating.

Example Drill for Evacuating Your Home:

1. On the designated day, pretend you must leave your home fast due to a tsunami, wildfire, flood, hurricane, or chemical spill.
2. Grab your Go-Bags and go to your designated vehicle.
3. Is there anyone you need to help?
4. Who will remember pets?
5. Decide on a pet-friendly hotel outside of town. If you have the means, plan to stay there for the evening.
6. Use your emergency supplies to prepare meals.
7. Practice personal hygiene using the kit.
8. Listen to the weather radio.
9. Review emergency situations and diagrams in this book, *Disaster Ready*.
10. Play cards or some other form of entertainment.
11. In the morning, eat and drink from your kit.
12. Practice personal hygiene using the kit.
13. Discuss what went well and what you could improve. Take notes of any items in your emergency kit that need replenishing or updating.
14. Return to your home.

By participating in these biannual mock scenarios, you are not only maintaining the readiness of your emergency shelter, but also helping your family members or roommates be prepared for unforeseen situations while adding a fun and educational aspect to the process.

In the next chapter, you'll put all your learning together in one comprehensive plan and also celebrate how far you've come!

FIGURE 11.1: Bi-Annual Emergency Plan Drill

(Canvenia, 2023)

---

our FAMILY EMERGENCY PLAN
EMERGENCY PLAN DRILL

FAMILY: YEAR:

SPRING	**DATE:** **We completed our Fire Drill** ◯ **WHAT WE DID:** Evacuate / Shelter-in-Place **WHAT WE LEARNED:** **MOST MEMORABLE:** Shelter-in-Place Kit is Updated ◯ Portable Kit is Updated ◯
FALL	**DATE:** **We completed our Fire Drill** ◯ **WHAT WE DID:** Evacuate / Shelter-in-Place **WHAT WE LEARNED:** **MOST MEMORABLE:** Shelter-in-Place Kit is Updated ◯ Portable Kit is Updated ◯

Our Emergency Plan - Page 5 of 5

The Plan: Pulling It Together

"Promise me you'll always remember: You're braver than you believe, and stronger than you seem, and smarter than you think." (Christopher Robin to Pooh)

– by A.A. Milne, *Winnie the Pooh*

Action Items

- ✓ Review and celebrate your accomplishments.
- ✓ Identify special considerations for family members (babies, children, self, pets, etc.).
- ✓ Consider shutting off utilities for hurricanes or tropical storms.
- ✓ Learn when and how to reinforce your home.

REVIEWING YOUR ACCOMPLISHMENTS

By this time, you've gathered your resources and created your emergency kits. Look over the list below. Is there anything you have not done? If so, please revisit your Family Emergency Plan to make sure you complete it.

- ✓ You completed a fire-escape plan and reviewed it with your family or roommates. (Family Emergency Plan, Page 1.)
- ✓ You listed your family members' contact information, identified safe places and routes to them, and identified an emergency contact outside. (Family Emergency Plan, Page 2 .)
- ✓ You have listed medical conditions, medication schedules for all members (including pets) and contact information for health care providers. (Family Emergency Plan, Page 3.)
- ✓ You have listed insurance information and other support resources. (Family Emergency Plan, Page 4.)
- ✓ You have considered when you want to perform your first drill. (Family Emergency Plan, Page 5.)
- ✓ You have attached a picture of each family member, including any pets to your plan.
- ✓ You have made a copy of your Family Emergency Plan and placed it in your Car Kit.
- ✓ You have placed your Family Emergency Plan in your Go-Bag.
- ✓ You have created a space for your Go-Bag and extra water supply to be stored in a place that is easy to access.
- ✓ You have planned for your sensitive documents, having a place for them that is easy to access.

SPECIAL CONSIDERATIONS

Some family members may have additional needs, such as necessary medical equipment. Be sure to include any such equipment and medical needs in your Family Emergency Plan. Below are some medical issues to think about:

1. **People with Developmental or Intellectual Disabilities:**
   a. Electronic device with spare batteries for entertainment
   b. Sheets and cord to make a tent-like area to decrease stimulation
   c. Comfort foods

   (CDC, 2023, Children and Youth with Special Healthcare Needs in Emergencies)

2. **People who are deaf or hard of hearing:**
   a. Weather radio with text display and flashing alert
   b. Pen and paper

3. **People who are blind or have low vision:**
   a. Mark supplies with braille or large print
   b. Communication tools

4. **People with Alzheimer's Disease or Dementia:**
   a. Bring/pack items of familiarity

   b. Don't leave the person alone

   c. Seek a quiet corner/space

5. **People with mobility issues:**

   a. If an electric chair is used, have a backup manual wheelchair

   b. Keep an extra mobility device handy, such as a cane

(Ready.gov, 2023, People with Disabilities)

CHILDREN AT SCHOOL

Reuniting with a child who is at school during a local disaster requires careful planning and communication between family members and the school. Familiarize yourself with the school's emergency evacuation procedures and policies. Schools often have well-established plans for various types of disasters. Trust that the school staff will prioritize the safety of your child and try to follow their procedures.

CURRENT EMERGENCY CONTACT INFORMATION

At this point in the book, you have written your emergency contact list. Be sure that both the school and your family have updated emergency contact information for each other. This should include phone numbers, email addresses, and alternative contacts if the primary ones are unreachable.

COMMUNICATION DURING THE DISASTER

Stay informed about the situation through local news, radio, or official government channels. Follow emergency alerts and instructions from local authorities. Attempt to contact the school through its emergency communication channels (if available) to check on the safety and status of your child. Be patient, as the school may be overwhelmed with inquiries during a disaster.

If it is safe to do so and you're not under evacuation orders, you can try to go to the school once the disaster situation allows. However, avoid interfering with emergency responders. Communicate with the school and follow its instructions regarding the timing and location for picking up your child. They may have specific procedures in place.

When you arrive at the school, follow any designated assembly or reunification points. Be patient and prepared for some delay, as schools prioritize the orderly and safe release of students to authorized individuals. Bring proper identification and documentation to prove your identity and relationship to the child.

Safety should always be your top priority. If local authorities advise against traveling to the school or if road conditions are hazardous, try to follow their guidance and wait until it's safe to proceed. Having a well-thought-out family emergency plan and staying informed are key to ensuring a successful reunion with your child during a local disaster.

ELDERLY CARE

If you have an elderly member of your family, it's of great importance to plan for how you would care for them in the event of an emergency, whether with them or remotely. The following scenario will provide you with some tips on this topic.

Scenario of Evacuation for an Elderly Person Who Lives in a Home Alone

Mrs. Smith is an elderly woman who lives alone in a rural area prone to wildfires. In this scenario, local emergency services monitor weather conditions and fire risks. When the authorities detect an approaching wildfire, they issue evacuation orders and alerts through various channels, including:

1. Emergency Alert Systems: Mrs. Smith has registered for emergency alerts, which are sent through text messages, phone calls, or emergency notification apps on her smartphone.

2. Local News and Radio: Emergency information is broadcast on local news channels and radio stations.

3. Door-to-Door Notifications: Local volunteers or community emergency response teams may visit Mrs. Smith's home to ensure she receives the evacuation notice.

Assistance from Family and Neighbors: Mrs. Smith's family, who live in a nearby town, are aware of her situation and have a plan in place to assist her during emergencies. They receive the same evacuation alerts from the local authorities and initiate their response accordingly:

1. Family Communication: Mrs. Smith's family members contact her immediately to make sure she is aware of the evacuation order.

2. Transportation: They arrange for her evacuation by coordinating with local authorities or community organizations for transportation. If possible, they may come to pick her up themselves.

3. Neighbor assistance: Mrs. Smith maintains good relationships with her neighbors, who have also been informed about her circumstances. They assist her by helping pack essential items and providing emotional support.

Special Considerations: Given Mrs. Smith's age and potential mobility issues, there are some special considerations:

1. Mobility Equipment: Mrs. Smith uses a walker for mobility. She keeps her walker accessible and ensures it's in good working condition. She also has a lightweight folding wheelchair for longer distances or when her walker is not practical.

2. Medications and Medical Supplies: She maintains a personal emergency kit, which includes a supply of necessary medications, medical records, and essential medical supplies for managing her chronic health conditions.

3. Personal Identification: Mrs. Smith keeps important documents, such as her ID, insurance information, and a list of emergency contacts, in a waterproof bag within her emergency kit.

4. Communication Plan: Mrs. Smith has a designated family contact and a backup contact for communication during emergencies. They check in with her regularly during the evacuation to make sure she is safe and well.

5. Emotional Support: Family and neighbors are aware of the emotional impact of evacuations on elderly individuals. They offer comfort and reassurance to Mrs. Smith to help her reduce stress and anxiety.

By having a well-thought-out evacuation plan, a personal emergency kit, and a support network in place, Mrs. Smith is well-prepared for a wildfire or other threatening conditions. This preparedness provides her safety and peace of mind during a potentially stressful situation.

SHUTTING OFF UTILITIES FOR EARTHQUAKES, HURRICANES OR TROPICAL STORMS, AND NUCLEAR DISASTERS

Utilities can be your friend, even when they don't work. Both water and gas demand respect, and if you give it, you will be stronger as you face a disaster. Know when and how to turn off gas and water (Ready.gov, 2023, Safety Skills).

Before a hurricane or tropical storm, the CDC recommends, "If you have time, turn off the gas, electricity, and water" (CDC, 2023, Preparing for a Hurricane or Other Tropical Storm). Water was the subject of conversation during Step 7, and you can return to that chapter to find information on how to collect water. If you need to leave your home and wish to safeguard it from potential water damage, you can turn off the water valve located nearest to the point where your home's water pipe enters. If you are leaving during freezing conditions, you should consider leaving your sinks dripping to keep water moving, decreasing the chances the pipes will freeze (CDC, 2023, Extreme Cold).

GAS LEAKS OFTEN CAN BE STOPPED

Gas leaks are associated with increased fires and explosions after disasters (Ready.gov, 2023, Safety Skills), making the issue worth mentioning here. If you hear a hiss, smell the gas, or are instructed by authorities, you will want to know how to shut off the gas going to your home (if you have a single-family dwelling). Keep in mind, however, that turning it back on must only be done by a qualified professional, and it may take weeks for them to get there (FEMA, 2023, Preparing for Disaster).

NOW TO CONSIDER THE UNTHINKABLE

You have prepared and are ready for most disasters by this point in the book. With recent escalations of unrest and uncertainty in the world, let's consider how we would respond to a nuclear bomb or accident. Step 13 will familiarize you with some basic prepping for nuclear disasters.

STEP 13

Understanding Nuclear Disasters

"Courage is found in unlikely places," said Gildor.
"Be of good hope!"

– J.R.R. Tolkien, *The Fellowship of the Ring*

Action Items

- ✓ Understand how to shelter-in-place for nuclear disasters.
- ✓ Know how to decontaminate yourself and others.
- ✓ Consider adding a Potassium Iodide supplement to your kit.
- ✓ Consider including gas masks in your kit.

Preparing for a nuclear disaster requires special attention. While the likelihood of a nuclear disaster may be relatively low, it is a good idea to know how to respond in case such an event occurs. To give you some peace of mind: You already have your emergency kits, you already have your emergency plan, and you are already prepared for most disasters at this point!

BEING PREPARED FOR A NUCLEAR DISASTER

1. In the event of a nuclear disaster, general guidance is for you to "Get Inside, Stay Inside, and Stay Tuned" (CDC, 2023, What to Do: Get Inside).

2. The Blast Zone is represented by three zones within it: Severe Damage, Moderate Damage, and Light Damage (FEMA, 2022, Planning Guidance for Response to a Nuclear Detonation, Third Edition).

   a. The Severe Damage Zone is unlikely to have survivors.

   b. The Moderate Damage Zone will have "many serious injuries" as well as dangers, including fires, downed power lines, and unstable buildings. Evacuation may be immediately necessary if health conditions are serious and/or shelter is not readily available (FEMA, 2022, Planning Guidance for Response to a Nuclear Detonation, Third Edition).

   c. In the Light Damage Zone, almost all windows will be broken, resulting in injuries. Sheltering should be a priority when you are able to use your first aid kits to treat cuts and similar non-life-threatening injuries. You should also have a first aid kit in your vehicle, along with your emergency kit.

d. Outside the three noted Blast Zones, but within the region, nuclear fallout will occur at varying times, depending on the size of any ground explosion, the proximity of the disaster, and the direction of the wind (FEMA, 2022, Planning Guidance for Response to a Nuclear Detonation, Third Edition). If there is a nuclear explosion in your region you are expected to have minutes to find shelter, as the falling debris will be radiated (CDC, 2023, What to Do: Get Inside).

3. Finding shelter is the number-one response you need to remember (CDC, 2023, What to Do: Get Inside). Radiated particles will coat all outdoor things.

   a. Greater wall density, as found in materials like concrete or bricks, is advantageous. Basements surpass above-ground spaces in terms of safety. In multi-story buildings without basements, central locations are optimal, positioned far from exterior walls, the roof, and ground level, as radiated particles tend to accumulate in these areas (REMM, 2023, How Buildings Provide Shielding from a Nuclear Explosion).

   b. If you live in a trailer home or similar, small, above-ground home, consider knowing a nearby community center or church that has a basement that could be available for emergencies. Call your local emergency departments to learn more.

c. Turn off any air exchanger and cover any place where air can come in from outside. If you have it, use plastic sheeting and duct tape to help with this.

d. Expect to stay in the shelter for a minimum of 24 hours. Authorities will guide you via your emergency radio. If your radio does not work, 72 hours is a very safe guideline to protect yourself from radiation, but individual cases will depend on factors such as health conditions, access to resources, and safety.

4. Decontamination procedures are straightforward.

a. Don't leave people outside; help them by providing shelter (REMM, 2023, Fallout from a Nuclear Detonation: Description and Management).

b. After debris has begun to fall, try to help everyone who comes to your door (CDC, 2023, Radiation Emergencies).

c. See the Infographic (Figure 13.1) as developed by the Centers for Disease Control and Prevention (CDC) titled, "Decontamination for Yourself and Others." Reference to this infographic does not constitute endorsement or recommendation by the U.S. Government, Department of Health and Human Services, or Centers for Disease Control and Prevention. You may also find this infographic here: https://www.cdc.gov/nceh/radiation/emergencies/pdf/Infographic_Decontamination.pdf

FIGURE 13.1: CDC Infographic

(Centers for Disease Control and Prevention, 2023, Decontamination for Yourself and Others)

5. Potassium Iodide (KI) Supplement.

    a. This is a supplement that you may be advised to take after a nuclear incident. It "fills up" your thyroid so that nuclear iodine does not fill the space. Taking this supplement may decrease your risk for cancer (CDC, 2023, Frequently Asked Questions About a Nuclear Blast).

    b. Not all nuclear disasters involve radioactive iodine, so this is a prophylaxis that may or may not be indicated. You may purchase Potassium Iodide for your emergency kit, but authorities encourage you to wait for guidance at the time of any nuclear accident (WHO, 1999, Guidelines for Iodine Prophylaxis Following Nuclear Accidents).

    c. Contraindications for the use of stable iodine include a history of thyroid disease (such as active hyperthyroidism), known hypersensitivity to iodine, dermatitis herpetiformis, and hypocomplementaemic vasculitis (WHO, 1999, Guidelines for Iodine Prophylaxis Following Nuclear Accidents).

    d. According to the World Health Organization, "To protect against inhaled radioactive iodine, a single dose of stable iodine would generally be sufficient, as it gives adequate protection for one day" (WHO, 1999, Guidelines for Iodine Prophylaxis Following Nuclear Accidents).

e. To obtain full effectiveness of stable iodine for thyroidal blocking requires that it be administered shortly before exposure or as soon after as possible" (WHO, 1999, Guidelines for Iodine Prophylaxis Following Nuclear Accidents).

f. See the Appendix for resources, including supplies such as Potassium Iodide and Gas Masks

6. A Note About Respirators (Gas Masks).

a. If you must be outside, cover yourself as best possible. An N-95 mask is better than a handkerchief. You should have this type of mask in your emergency kit.

b. A gas mask for each family member is an extra layer of security and is especially helpful in the event chemicals become involved in any terrorist incident (CDC, 2023, Respirator Fact Sheet).

Remember that preparedness is key; and while the prospect of a nuclear disaster is unsettling, being well-informed and ready can make a significant difference in your safety and well-being. Follow the guidance of local authorities as information and resources unfold. Your analog emergency radio may be your most reliable source of information.

NUCLEAR DISASTER SCENARIOS

Scenario of Man Driving Between Towns

John was driving along a desolate stretch of highway, enjoying a peaceful ride back to the office. The sun was shining, and he had the windows down as his car cruised down the seemingly endless road. Suddenly, as he rounded a bend, his eyes widened at the sight of a massive mushroom cloud on the distant horizon, approximately 30 miles away. Panic set in as he realized it was a nuclear event. He knew he had to find shelter immediately.

With a racing heart and a mind filled with fear, John began to think about his shelter options:

1. **Abandoned Buildings**: As he scanned the landscape, he noticed an abandoned gas station up ahead. John considered pulling over and seeking shelter inside the concrete structure, but he knew it would be too small and not likely to have a basement.

2. **Underground Structures**: John remembered passing a small mining facility a few miles back. He thought about turning around and heading there, hoping that the

underground tunnels might shield him from the nuclear fallout.

3. **Culvert or Tunnel**: As he continued to drive, he spotted a large drainage culvert on the side of the road. He thought about parking his car there and taking shelter inside, but he knew he needed a shelter that would provide several feet of distance between him and the surface above him, and the space would need to be sealed with plastic. He kept driving.

4. **Vehicle Shelter**: John was aware that the small emergency kit in his car contained a mylar emergency blanket, some non-perishable food, and a few bottles of water. He remembered that the radioactive debris that would land on the surfaces of the car would be deadly close to him. Outdriving the fallout would be too risky.

5. **Local Community Center**: John had a vague memory of passing a small town a few miles back. He thought about heading there and seeking shelter in a community center or a local church, hoping that it might have a basement or other secure area that could serve as a makeshift fallout shelter.

As John weighed his options, he knew he had to make a quick decision. The distant mushroom cloud continued to loom ominously on the horizon, and the clock was ticking. He decided to head toward the town with the church, hoping it would be open to offer its basement for protection from the nuclear event. He sped toward the shelter, praying that he had made the right choice to survive the impending disaster. He reached for the small emergency kit in his car and grabbed the essentials. The door of the church was open. He ran to the basement and helped others by sharing his emergency radio and anticipating the next moves, such as turning off fans, sealing vents to the basement room, and getting prepared to decontaminate people as they arrived.

Scenario of 10-Year-Old in School

As the news of the nuclear event spread, John's thoughts were consumed with worry about his 10-year-old child back in their hometown, about 25 miles from the disaster. He knew that the school where his child attended had a well-established emergency plan in place, and they would be taking immediate action to ensure the safety of the students.

School Response to the Nuclear Event:

1. **Alert and Evacuation**: Upon receiving a warning or notification of the nuclear event, the school's emergency response team initiated its emergency plan. Teachers immediately gathered the students and evacuated them from outdoor areas, moving them to designated safe

locations inside the school building. They moved the children to a lower, inside area of the school, such as the basement or a reinforced interior room, to minimize exposure to radiation and protect them from falling debris.

2. **Communication with Families**:

- The school activated its communication system, which included automated calls, text messages, and emails to notify parents of the situation and reassure them that their children were safe.

- The school's website and social media channels were updated with real-time information about the event and the school's response.

- School staff also communicated with local authorities and emergency management agencies to stay updated on the situation and receive guidance.

John trusted the authorities to protect his son and to advise everyone of the next steps. He wondered how the school would manage families who arrive at the school while radioactive debris was falling, insisting on getting their children. He believed the radiation could kill them within days if the winds continued as they were. He hoped the school had a plan to take people into the school to shelter them.

Scenario of Medical Worker at Work

Samantha, a medical worker, was on her shift at the local hospital when news of the nuclear event broke out, about 45 miles away. As an experienced professional, she understood the gravity of the situation and was prepared to follow the hospital's emergency protocols to ensure the safety and care of her patients.

Samantha knew that the size of the bomb and the wind direction would be factors the specialists would be considering before issuing commands and guidance, but she anticipated many things. She knew that with a nuclear event so close, it may be important to avoid proximity to any walls or to the roof. Moving patients toward spaces near the center of the building would be important. She was aware that the hospital would likely be operating at an increased capacity for an extended period. She knew she would most likely have to stay indoors for at least 24, and maybe as much as 72 hours or longer, depending on the severity of the situation. She had prepared for emergencies before; she knew she might have to stay at the hospital for an extended period and had already discussed this possibility with her family. Samantha had a locker at work where she kept essential personal items, such as emergency contact information, medicine, toiletries, and a change of clothes. She was familiar with emergencies, but this one was different.

The hospital would soon be flooded with patients coming from the streets, seeking treatment for injuries or possible radiation exposure. She expected chaos in the emergency room and throughout the hospital, with medical teams working tirelessly to provide care to those in need. Samantha had heard that decontamination stations were being set up immediately to address potential contamination of patients and hospital staff. Specialized units within the hospital focused on managing the medical aspects related to radiation exposure and providing support to patients with radiation sickness.

As the situation unfolded, Samantha and her colleagues worked diligently to ensure that patients were relocated to safer areas within the hospital, that decontamination procedures were in place, and that everyone received the care they needed. The facilities department had ensured air exchangers were off and areas were sealed off. Despite the chaos and uncertainty, their commitment to their roles as medical professionals and the hospital's emergency preparedness helped them navigate the challenging circumstances and provide critical care during the nuclear event.

Scenario of a Medical Worker's Child at Daycare

Samantha found herself in a challenging situation during the nuclear event, not only due to her responsibilities at the hospital but also because her 6-year-old son, Alex, was at daycare. However, she had taken the time to prepare him for such situations through regular drills and discussions about emergency preparedness. Here's how she handled the situation:

1. **Daycare's Emergency Response Plan**: Samantha was confident that the daycare where Alex was located had a well-established emergency response plan. She had previously discussed it with the daycare staff, and they assured her that in the event of a disaster, the children would be contained in a secure basement shelter. The daycare's plan included monitoring broadcasted information and keeping parents/guardians informed about the status of their children via text messages and postings to a social media account.

2. **Trust in Preparedness Drills**: Over the years, Samantha had conducted bi-annual camping trips (drills) with Alex to prepare him for various emergency scenarios. During these "camp out" drills, they made it fun by using flashlights, listening to a weather radio, wearing masks, trying unusual meals, and practicing unique ways of washing and using the restroom. While

they would play games, they would talk about what would happen if he needed to stay at daycare because of something strange happening. These drills had not only educated Alex but also helped reduce his fear and anxiety associated with emergencies.

3. **Confidence in Alex's Preparedness**: Samantha had talked to Alex about what to do if they were separated during an emergency. She had taught him to listen to the daycare staff, stay calm, and follow instructions. She knew her son would miss her and be scared, but she was confident that the preparation and discussions they had shared would help him handle the situation better.

4. **Reassurance through Communication**: Samantha had explained to Alex that if they ever found themselves in a situation like this, she would do everything in her power to ensure he was safe and that they would be reunited as soon as possible. She reassured him that daycare was a safe place with adults who knew how to take care of the children.

Despite the difficult circumstances, Samantha's prior efforts in educating and preparing her son for emergencies helped alleviate some of the anxiety that Alex might have experienced. She knew that he was in capable hands at the daycare and that the drills they had practiced together had given him a sense of empowerment and confidence to face this disaster.

Scenario of a Retired Woman in a Retirement Cooperative

Eleanor, a retired woman living in a four-story retirement facility in the same community, had prepared for an emergency with the help of her daughter several months ago. Little did she know that her emergency plan and kit would soon become invaluable during the nuclear disaster.

As the news of the impending nuclear fallout reached her facility, she knew she had only minutes to prepare. Her daughter's guidance and the emergency plan they had crafted together became her lifeline in this moment of crisis. Eleanor made a critical decision: she opted to secure her second-story unit instead of heading to the small basement room with others, a choice driven by her desire to minimize the number of people in the crowded basement and maintain her independence. She knew her chosen location would be far away from the walls and roof, and she let her neighbor know what she was doing. Her neighbor headed to the basement.

Here's how Eleanor handled the emergency:

1. **Securing Her Second-Story Unit**: Eleanor quickly assessed her situation. She turned off her air exchanger to

prevent the intake of potentially contaminated air. She knew that sealing herself in a secure inner area of her second-story unit was a good option for protection against radiation and fallout.

2. **Gathering Emergency Kit Items**: She retrieved her emergency kit from the closet in the small office she used to write books, a room she had previously identified as her designated emergency shelter. The kit contained all her essential supplies, including non-perishable food, plenty of water, a flashlight, a battery-powered radio, first-aid supplies, and personal hygiene items.

3. **Preparing Her Shelter Area**: Eleanor unfolded a cot and laid out bedding in her emergency shelter. She made sure she had enough blankets and warm clothing to stay comfortable during the potentially extended stay.

4. **Maintaining Contact**: Eleanor had a charged cellphone with her and a portable charger (power bank), allowing her to maintain contact with her daughter and the outside world. Her over-protective daughter had also provided her with a walkie-talkie in her emergency kit in case the cellular network did not work. Eleanor was glad to have it.

5. **Waiting and Staying Informed**: In the safety of her makeshift shelter, Eleanor waited for updates and news about the nuclear event. She tuned into the hand-cranked, battery-powered radio to listen to emergency broadcasts and stay informed about the situation. Just as she figured, her cell phone did not let her call her daughter. She sent a text reporting her well-being, turned on her walkie-talkie, and read a book.

Eleanor's decision to secure her own space and rely on her carefully prepared emergency kit worked well. Over the next 72 hours, she remained in her shelter, occasionally communicating with her daughter via text messages and receiving updates on the situation via her emergency radio. It turned out the walkie-talkie channels were also congested, so she and her daughter planned to turn them on at two specific times each day. While it was a tense and challenging experience, Eleanor's preparations and her choice to stay in her second-story unit contributed to her safety and well-being during the nuclear disaster.

The final step in becoming *Disaster Ready* is to share your newfound knowledge with others!

"In time of test, family is best."
– Burmese Proverb

Before you continue to your 14th step, please consider leaving a review on Amazon, as it helps us spread the word! They, too, can Be Disaster Ready in 14 Steps!

http://bit.ly/DisasterReadyin14Steps

Share Your Knowledge Preemptively

"You can't stay in your corner of the forest waiting for others to come to you. You have to go to them sometimes."

— A.A. Milne, *Winnie the Pooh*

ACTION ITEMS:

- ✓ Encourage a neighbor to get prepared. You will be stronger if you have a community in that day of need.
- ✓ Share your knowledge with them.
- ✓ Consider taking a First Aid or other useful class to continue learning about emergency preparedness.

BECOME VALUABLE TO YOUR NEIGHBORS

All you have learned up to this point is foundational. I hope you are proud of your accomplishments and celebrate by rewarding yourself in some way. When you are ready, I challenge you to present yourself to your neighborhood as a valuable person to know. When food and resources are scarce, you want to be valuable to people. A link to a free PDF download, titled,

"*Investing in Skills for Survival: a guided journal,*" is at the end of this book.

> "*The best investment you can make*
> *is in yourself (in your skills).*"
> – Warren Buffett

NEIGHBORHOOD WATCH AND COMMUNITY GROUPS

Local groups can provide an easy way to share information. If they prepare themselves for a disaster, you will be stronger as well. Similarly, if they have not prepared, and they do not have enough food or water, will you be able to help? By acting preemptively, you will help your neighbors be thoughtful about their situation. Below is a template you can use to invite them to join the movement to be stronger through preparation.

FIGURE 14.1: Invitation for Neighbors

(Canvenia, 2023)

SIMPLY PREPARED

Dear

I live at _____

I have been learning about being ready for any disaster and have prepared myself in some basic ways. Here are some skills I have in case you need help:

I can

_____

_____

_____

_____

_____

If you would like to learn more about preparing for disasters, below is a QR code to a book that helped me prepare.

[QR Code will go here]

Disaster Ready in 14 Steps: Emergency Survival Guide for New Preppers (available on Amazon)

Kind regards,

Printed Name:

Phone Number:

Conclusion

You are ready. You have a plan, kits, and you know how to use them. Now enjoy your family and friends.

> *"There are far, far better things ahead than any we leave behind."*

> – C.S. Lewis

If you haven't already, please consider leaving a review on Amazon. It can help others Be Disaster Ready in 14 Steps!

Appendix

TEMPLATE FOR PETS

PET EMERGENCY KIT

_____ Water
_____ Food
_____ Medicine
_____ Blanket (light weight)
_____ Dish for Water/Food

Pet Litter/Box/Newspaper/Bleach _____
First Aid Kit _____
Toy _____
Travelling Carrier or Crate _____
Backup Leash _____

SPECIAL CONSIDERATIONS

Pet-friendly hotels: _____

_____

_____

Friends/Family/Shelters: _____

_____

_____

Index

References

AAA (2015). Tire Inflator Kits Fact Sheet. Retrieved October 29, 2023, from https://newsroom.aaa.com/wp-content/uploads/2019/06/Tire-Inflator-Kit-Fact-Sheet-FINAL.pdf

Canvenia (2023). Infographics. Retrieved October 31, 2023, from Canvenia.com.

Centers for Disease Control and Prevention (CDC) (2023). Be Ready for Radiation Emergencies. Retrieved October 19, 2023, from https://www.cdc.gov/nceh/features/beready

Centers for Disease Control and Prevention (CDC) (2023). Children and Youth with Special Healthcare Needs in Emergencies. Retrieved October 23, 2023, from https://www.cdc.gov/childrenindisasters/children-with-special-healthcare-needs.html

Centers for Disease Control and Prevention (CDC) (2023). Extreme Cold. Retrieved October 30, 2023, https://www.cdc.gov/disasters/winter/pdf/extreme-cold-guide.pdf

Centers for Disease Control and Prevention (CDC) (2023). Frequently Asked Questions About a Nuclear Blast.

Retrieved November 12, 2023 from
https://www.cdc.gov/nceh/radiation/emergencies/nucle
arfaq.htm

Centers for Disease Control and Prevention (CDC) (2023). How
to Self-Decontaminate after a Radiation Emergency.
Retrieved November 11, 2023, from
https://www.cdc.gov/nceh/radiation/emergencies/selfde
con_wash.htm

Centers for Disease Control and Prevention (CDC) (2023).
Infographic: Decontamination for Yourself and Others.
Retrieved November 11, 2023 from
https://www.cdc.gov/nceh/radiation/emergencies/pdf/I
nfographic_Decontamination.pdf

Centers for Disease Control and Prevention (CDC) (2023). Make
Water Safe During an Emergency.
https://www.cdc.gov/healthywater/emergency/pdf/mak
e-water-safe-during-emergency-p.pdf Retrieved October
18, 2023, from
https://www.cdc.gov/healthywater/emergency/making-
water-safe.html

Centers for Disease Control and Prevention (CDC) (2023).
Preparing for a Hurricane. Retrieved October 23, 2023,

from
https://www.cdc.gov/disasters/hurricanes/before.html

Centers for Disease Control and Prevention (CDC) (2023).
#PrepYourHealth to Drive During Winter. Retrieved
October 29, 2023, from
https://blogs.cdc.gov/publichealthmatters/2023/01/win
ter-driving/

Centers for Disease Control and Prevention (CDC) (2023).
Radiation Emergencies. Retrieved October 19, 2023,
from https://www.cdc.gov/nceh/radiation/emergencies/
index.htm

Centers for Disease Control and Prevention (CDC) (2023).
Respirator Fact Sheet. Retrieved November 14, 2023,
from
https://www.cdc.gov/niosh/npptl/topics/respirators/fac
tsheets/respfact.html

Centers for Disease Control and Prevention (CDC) (2023). Stay
Safe During & After a Winter Storm. Retrieved October
29, 2023, from
https://www.cdc.gov/disasters/winter/duringstorm/ind
oorsafety.html

Centers for Disease Control and Prevention (CDC) (2023).
Water Disinfection. Retrieved October 19, 2023, from

https://wwwnc.cdc.gov/travel/yellowbook/2024/preparing/water-disinfection

Centers for Disease Control and Prevention (CDC) (2023). What to Do: Get Inside. Retrieved November 6, 2023, from https://www.cdc.gov/nceh/radiation/emergencies/getinside.htm

County of Alameda, California (2023). Emergency Water. Retrieved October 23, 2023, from https://www.acgov.org/ready/documents/EmergencyDrinkingWaterHandout.pdf

Dr. Seuss, *Oh, the Places You'll Go!,* Retrieved October 30, 2023, from goodreads.com

EPA (See United States Environmental Protection Agency)

Federal Emergency Management Agency (FEMA) (2023). Preparing for Disaster. Retrieved October 23, 2023, from https://www.fema.gov/pdf/library/pfd.pdf

J.R.R. Tolkien, *The Fellowship of the Ring.* Retrieved October 30, 2023, from goodreads.com.

Loma Linda University (2023). Emergency Food. Retrieved October 28, 2023, from https://llu.edu/campus-spiritual-life/emergency/emergency-food

Radiation Emergency Medical Management (REMM) (2023). Fallout from a Nuclear Detonation: Description and Management. Retrieved November 9, 2023 from https://remm.hhs.gov/nuclearfallout.htm

Radiation Emergency Medical Management (REMM) (2023). How Buildings Provide Shielding from a Nuclear Explosion. Retrieved November 9, 2023 from https://remm.hhs.gov/buildingblast.htm

Ready.gov (2023). Prepare Your Pets for Disasters. Retrieved October 18,2023, from https://www.ready.gov/pets

Ready.gov (2023). People with Disabilities. Retrieved October 23, 2023, from https://www.ready.gov/disability

Ready.gov (2023). Safety Skills. Retrieved October 19, 2023, from https://www.ready.gov/safety-skills

Red Cross (2023). Frozen Pipes. Retrieved October 27, 2023, from https://www.redcross.org/get-help/how-to-prepare-for-emergencies/types-of-emergencies/winter-storm/frozen-pipes.html

Red Cross (2023). Home Fire Safety. Retrieved October 29, 2023, from https://www.redcross.org/get-help/how-to-prepare-for-emergencies/types-of-emergencies/fire.html

Red Cross (2023). Survival Kit Supplies. Retrieved October 22, 2023, from https://www.redcross.org/get-help/how-to-prepare-for-emergencies/survival-kit-supplies.html

Simms, Chris (2023). Occam's razor. *New Scientist*. Retrieved October 29, 2023, from https://www.newscientist.com/definition/occams-razor

United States Environmental Protection Agency (EPA) (2023). Power Outages and Indoor Air Quality (IAQ). Retrieved October 27, 2023, from https://www.epa.gov/indoor-air-quality-iaq/power-outages-and-indoor-air-quality-iaq#safely

Wien M, Sabaté J. Food selection criteria for disaster response planning in urban societies. Nutr J. 2015 May 12; 14:47. doi: 10.1186/s12937-015-0033-0. PMID: 25962636; PMCID: PMC4489367. Retrieved October 28, 2023, from https://www.ncbi.nlm.nih.gov/pmc/articles/PMC4489367/

World Health Organization, 1999, Guidelines for Iodine Prophylaxis Following Nuclear Accidents. Retrieved November 11, 2023 from https://iris.who.int/bitstream/handle/10665/66143/WHO_SDE_PHE_99.6.pdf

Resources

Below are resources for you to consider as you collect items for your kits. Our family has purchased many of these items. You will not need everything listed. Use the list to learn options you have. The items are almost exclusively links to products on Amazon, so you will not be sent in 10 different directions at this early stage. Pre-made kits may be useful to you, and Amazon has a wide selection. Your local stores will have many items also.

Disclosure: The links to Amazon are affiliate links, meaning our family receives a small benefit from purchases at no additional cost to you.

EMERGENCY KITS

Adult Kits

Urban Survival Bug-Out Bag. 72-Hour Emergency Kit. 5-year shelf life. USA-made SOS food ration bars. (4-person kit). https://amzn.to/407Ne6g

Family Prep 72-Hour Survival Kit/Go-Bag. 72-hour supply, 5-year shelf life. USA-made SOS food ration bars. (2- and 4-person kits). https://amzn.to/3tKY329

Youth Kits

Children's Deluxe 72-Hour Emergency Survival Kit. Includes USA-made SOS food ration bars and water with a 5-year shelf life. https://amzn.to/46LVV8P

Pet Kits

Dogs

Pet Emergency Kit for Big Dogs. 72-hour supply, 5-year shelf life. (Pet Evak Pak). 48 pieces. https://amzn.to/45INn1f

Pet Emergency Kit for 2 Big Dogs. 72-hour supply, 5-year shelf life. (Pet Evak Pak). https://amzn.to/3MbkWSF

Pet Emergency Kit for Medium Dogs. 72-hour supply, 5-year shelf life. (Pet Evak Pak). https://amzn.to/4O7OoTX

Pet Emergency Kit for Small Dog - in Cinch Bag. 72-hour supply, 5-year shelf life. (Pet Evak Pak). https://amzn.to/45GGHAD

Cats

Cat Emergency Kit for Cats - in Cinch Bag. 5-year shelf life. (Pet Evak Pak). https://amzn.to/3FpCTsO

Ultimate Emergency Kit for Cats - with Carrier. 72-hour supply, 5-year shelf life. (Pet Evak Pak). https://amzn.to/3rVDiQP

Dog & Cat Combo: Pet Emergency Kit. (Pet Evak Pak). https://amzn.to/3sozD3Y

Food Kits

Freeze Dried Food Kits. Many of these kits have a shelf life of up to 25 years. These can be nice if you have a means to heat water. There are many choices. If you have any allergies, be sure to review the ingredients lists. You can see a large selection here: https://amzn.to/3M9ogxJ

Toileting Kit

Sanitation Set with Privacy Shelter. Hygienic Waste Disposal System for Camping, Hiking, Emergency Preparedness. https://amzn.to/3QwjVr2

MISC SUPPLIES

Emergency Radio, Flashlight, and Charges Cell Phones:

Hand Crank Emergency/Weather Radio with Port to

Charge Cell Phone (also has flashlight and solar charger). A similar device is included in kits (above). https://amzn.to/3Sa3qlG

Cooking, Boiling Water, and Charging Cell Phones:

Biolite Campstove with phone charging port. Wood Burning, Electricity Generating & USB Charging Camp Stove, Complete Cook Kit: This is expensive, but lightweight and allows for boiling water with minimal wood; also charges cell phones. This is for outdoor use only. https://amzn.to/3QnmcEC

SUPPLIES FOR NUCLEAR DISASTERS

Medicine: Potassium Iodide

Radiation Tablets 130 mg - (60 Tablets) EXP 10/2032 – Anti Nuclear Fallout Pills – Made in the USA.

Instructions are provided on the bottle and by authorities in the event this medicine could help you: https://amzn.to/41kYOM5

Gas Masks

MIRA SAFETY M CBRN Full Face Reusable Respirator-Mask & drinking system. Many sizes, including for kids. https://amzn.to/3s5zqwE

Filter for 40 mm Gas Masks: Israeli Gas Mask Filter Nato Specifications NBC for 40mm Gas Masks. **25-year shelf life.** https://amzn.to/3FtjPKs

There's More!

If you liked this publication, download our FREE eBook of the season at the URL below. At the time of publication, the free PDF download is:

5 for 2024: Investing in Skills for Survival – a Guided Journal
www.Canvenia.com/Simply-Prepared-Gift

Help us teach more people to become prepared!
Please leave a Review!

http://bit.ly/DisasterReadyin14Steps

Thank You!

Made in the USA
Las Vegas, NV
22 December 2023

83440619R00098